COSTA BLANCA CLIMBS
Including
MAJORCA

An Introductory Guide

After a hard morning on the crag

COSTA BLANCA
CLIMBS

Including
MAJORCA

An Introductory Guide

by

Chris Craggs

Cicerone Press
Milnthorpe, Cumbria

ISBN 1 85284 058 7

ACKNOWLEDGEMENTS

Many thanks to Dave, Mike, Jim and Colin for some great days in the sun, and for their help and encouragement on and off the rock. Special thanks to Graham without whose talents the contents of this book would be somewhat thinner and a lot easier, and to Sherri who looked after all of us and who always insisted Spain would be a great place to visit.
She was right.

Front cover: Via Missing Link (E3 5c) Toix Sea Cliff New Year's Eve 1988. Where were you?
Back Cover: Colin Binks on Graphic Whore (E3 6a) Toix E

CONTENTS

INTRODUCTION

A recent publication by the World Health Organisation described the Costa Blanca as having "perhaps the most ideal climate in the World." Certainly to those of us brought up on our own damp and foggy group of islands, the lure of winter sun is a powerful magnet. When you add to this cheap charter flights to the area, masses of low priced accommodation and inexpensive food and drink, the place sounds almost too good to be true. Then of course there is the rock climbing. Where the Sierra de Bernia runs into the Mediterranean there is an impressive series of headlands and gorges. Tucked between these are the white beaches so beloved of the tourist brochures that give the area its name. The cliffs vary in size from less than 50 feet to over a thousand feet, and vary in quality from perfect grey limestone to vertical grot, fortunately with the former predominating.

The development has gone through two distinct phases. Firstly the larger, more impressive cliffs were developed in the alpine tradition, with the major lines being tackled and aid being used as and when required. Secondly, the smaller roadside crags have been equipped with short, safe and sometimes hard routes. This second phase of development is still in full swing with new routes and whole new cliffs being discovered. There is so much rock in the area that it will be many years before it is worked out. So there really is something here for everybody, from a couple of weeks of rocking to the odd route grabbed while the family are left on the beach.

When To Go

The Mediterranean summers are hot to very hot and only the most dedicated 'hot rock jocks' will be capable of coping. Also at this time the area is crowded and the prices inflated. On the other hand, the autumn to spring season has a lot of advantages. Accommodation is freely available and very reasonably priced, from basic apartments to luxury villas complete with swimming pools. Charter flights from the U.K. are inexpensive, especially if the school holidays can be

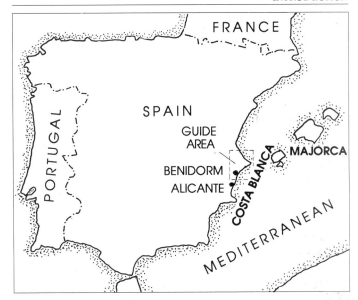

avoided. The evenings are cool and daytime temperatures are often agreeably warm without the humidity that we usually associate with heat. Oranges, olives and almonds are all ready for harvesting and the bird life (feathered variety) is very un-British. Winter rains can occur and are most common in February, though a bad Spanish winter is usually better than a good English summer. As the spring progresses the blossom appears on the trees, lemons, apricots and artichokes ripen and the weather warms up. With this there is often an increase in humidity with a consequent increased risk of thunderstorms (usually short-lived affairs). June to September are hot, dry and crowded. Despite this a climbing holiday can still be enjoyed by choosing routes in the shade, although rather more time may have to be spent on the beach or in the pool - how sad!

How To Get There and Where To Stay
Any travel agent should be able to fix you up with a reasonably priced flight from your local airport, though it is certainly worth

7

shopping around. A few phone calls to any of the numbers in the Sunday papers may pay dividends. If at all possible it is worth arriving around midday to allow time for orientation and organisation. Hire cars are amongst the cheapest in Europe and are best booked from the U.K. They can be picked up and left at any time of day or night; most of the companies are used to strange arrival and departure times.

Camping or bivvying is all really unnecessary unless it turns you on. There are plenty of companies that arrange a whole variety of accommodation - consult your travel agent or the Sunday press. Calpe is the ideal base, though the whole coast from Denia in the north down to Altea and Benidorm in the south are peppered with villa developments. Any of these would be an acceptable place to stay, within 30 minutes drive of most of the climbing.

From Alicante airport the quickest way to get to Calpe is to follow signs for VALENCIA and the A7. Once through Alicante the motorway gives an easy 45 kilometre drive through scenery that gradually becomes more impressive. At the present time the toll is just over 500 pesetas. Leave the motorway at Altea and turn north. Calpe is 11 kilometres away just beyond the Mascarat Gorge.

For those who made no prior arrangements concerning accommodation the Tourist Office in Calpe is very helpful, and will be able to fix you up with something suitable. The office is to be found on the main dual carriageway past the town, Avenue Ejercitos Espaniols, opposite the salt pans.

A Bit About The Climbing

All of the cliffs in this guide are composed of limestone. The rock is extremely rough and can rapidly make a mess of hands that have grown soft from a few months of inactivity (it also can play havoc with the most expensive of lycra). The majority of the routes are very well protected with bolts, often of a chain link variety and these are often spray painted with large coloured spots. This is ecologically a trifle insensitive as the biggest spots can be seen from hundreds of metres away, but at least it cuts down on route finding problems. On these routes (unless otherwise stated) the only equipment that is required is the appropriate number of quickdraws/crabs plus a pair

8

of 50 metre ropes and a descender (many of the pitches are longer than 25 metres, so lowering off "a la France" is often not possible).

On the longer routes a light British rack - rocks 1 to 9 and a couple of medium-sized Friends, plus a few slings for threads, are useful to supplement the often rather spaced in situ pegs.

The well tried and tested adjectival/"E" grades coupled with a technical grade have been used throughout. If there has been any doubt about the grade of a route I have erred on the side of safety by overgrading rather than undergrading (Holiday Grades). All these grades assume an on-site flash of the appropriate route whether it be VS or E6. No allowances have been made for dogging, frogging, frigging or any other methods of bringing the route down to a person's own level of ability. If you find all the routes easier than expected it is obviously a measure of your talent rather than anything amiss with the system!

A one to three star system has been used as an indicator of relative merit, though all the routes included in the guide are worth doing

I have adopted a rather novel concept of describing horizontal distances in metric units and vertical distances in imperial units. The logic (flawed as it may be) behind this idea is that all the road signs are in kilometres but most climbers still think vertically in feet, (I have yet to hear anyone say, "there is a good jug 80cm to your right" or "you can get a good rest at 18m"). If you find this system a little off-putting just divide the feet by three, (on the other hand if you are a dyed in the wool Empire man multiply the metres by three).

A Warning! Ignore At Your Peril!
Car thieves operate in this area. Small hire cars are no challenge to them; they will break the lock or window as is necessary to get at anything (or anything that appears to be hidden) in the car. Leave **NOTHING** in the car and leave the glove box open. If you do have a break-in be warned - the local police do not speak English and they require the filling in of reams of paper work. It's best to avoid the hassle.

The climbing areas are described from south to north progressing up the coast, but for each crag the approaches are taken from Calpe.

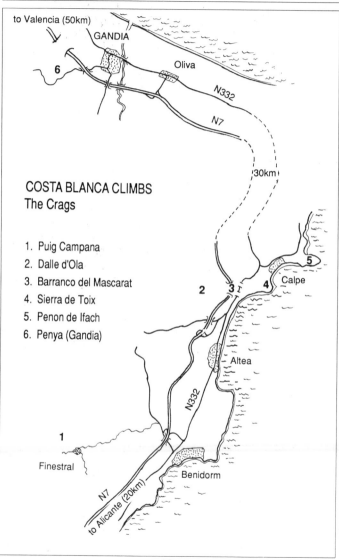

COSTA BLANCA CLIMBS
The Crags

1. Puig Campana
2. Dalle d'Ola
3. Barranco del Mascarat
4. Sierra de Toix
5. Penon de Ifach
6. Penya (Gandia)

to Valencia (50km)

GANDIA

Oliva

N332

N7

30km

Calpe

Altea

N332

Finestral

Benidorm

N7

to Alicante (20km)

PUIG CAMPANA 1406m

As you travel northwards on the motorway the Puig Campana is the first of the larger mountains that appears on your left. It is instantly recognisable because of the great square notch missing from the summit ridge.

Character
The routes described are to be found on the south face of the mountain. They are generally not of a great level of difficulty, in the range severe to E2, but are a respectable length (4 to 8 pitches) and are in a remote setting - not a sensible place to have an accident. There is rather a dearth of fixed gear on the routes so carry a light to average U.K. rack, depending on your level of confidence/foolhardiness. The approach walk will deter many but the climbing is worth the slight effort involved. A water bottle, at least at the start of the climbs is worth considering.

Approach
The walk-in starts at Finestrat which is reached by turning inland from the Benidorm exit on the motorway. The village is reached in 8 kilometres. Once in Finestrat follow signs to the Font de Moli (a well). 150 metres past the well take a left turn and follow this road until it is possible to park just past a bridge over a dry (usually!) river bed. From here a gravel track leads northwards towards the mountain. The red paint flecks mark the walking route to the summit via the great gully in the south face - a worthwhile day out. This path is followed until it is possible to walk leftwards underneath the south face. Most of the climbs have their names painted discreetly at the foot of the route (DIEDRE MAGICS is the exception). The approach time is about 45 minutes to an hour.

To reach the first route described continue along below the face until the terrace ends. Scramble up and leftwards over a 30ft rocky step to reach the basin between the south ridge and the south-west face. The climb starts at a slabby groove (cairn) at the upper right

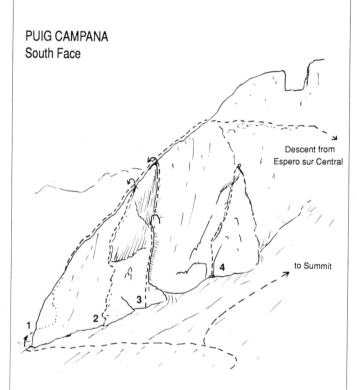

PUIG CAMPANA
South Face

Descent from
Espero sur Central

to Summit

1. Espero Sur Central / from Finestrat
2. Via Julia
3. Diedre Gallego
4. Diedre Magics

corner of the basin.

ESPERO SUR CENTRAL *** Severe c1200ft.
A long and interesting route following a fine mountain feature. Technical difficulties are low so the situations can be enjoyed to the full.
1.   90ft.   Follow the slabby groove and move right to a belay on a long ledge system.
2.   100ft.   Walk along the ledge rightwards until below another groove.
3.   140ft.   Up the groove to another ledge system which is followed to the right until below (you guessed it) a third groove.
4.   80ft.   This groove is a little meatier than the lower ones and leads to an open belay on the ridge crest. Good views across the south face.
5.   130ft.   Follow the crest of the ridge on superb rock to a belay on a small ledge.
6.   150ft.   Move a few feet left of the ridge into a long open corner, at its top climb up and right to a good ledge back on the crest.
7.   140ft.   Again traverse up and left to gain access to a corner which leads to a break in the ridge.
8.   130ft.   Above lies the crux, another groove on the crest, with perhaps a move of 4a. If this proves too much the crack to the left is somewhat easier.
9.   100ft.   Continue up the ridge, now easier angled until a steep step leads to an open corner.
10. 100ft.   The climbing now eases as height is gained.

This is the end of the technical rock climbing. For the DESCENT continue up the easy angled ridge until it steepens up in an obvious headwall. Traverse to the right (cairns) to a short slabby barrier of rock. Up this (Diff) to a path that leads down rightwards into the South Gully which was passed on the approach to the cliff. 30-60 minutes from the end of the climbing.

VIA JULIA ** E1 600ft.

One of the shortest routes on the face and offering varied climbing. It takes the centre of the face bounded on the left by the south ridge and on the right by the great groove line of DIEDRE GALLEGO. Start midway between the arête and the groove line.

1.   150ft.   4b.   Climb straight up to the small overhang which is passed on the left to get into a corner. This leads to a good ledge with a belay to the left.

2.   150ft.   5b.   Above is a long crack system, this is followed and gives a strenuous and sustained pitch to a stance on top of a pillar.

3.   150ft.   5a.   Traverse 10ft left then climb directly up the face passing an awkward overhang at 40ft. Eventually a slanting groove leads to a stance almost on the arête. It is possible to escape down (or up!) ESPERO CENTRAL at this point.

4.   150ft.   5b.   The slanting crack to the right is followed easily until it rears up. More difficult climbing leads to a stance on the ridge crest.

DESCENT. Cross over the arête and descend 30ft to find abseil anchors. A 140ft abseil lands on a good ledge. Follow this rightwards (facing out) for 100ft and scramble down to another ledge with fixed threads. An 80ft abseil from these leads to a ledge which is followed to the right to a final short abseil. (This lower section is ESPERO CENTRAL in reverse.) From the foot of the abseils traverse to the left (looking out) passing below the arête back to the approach path.

VIA DIEDRE GALLEGO ** E2 640ft.

This route takes the striking groove line that soars up the centre of the south face. The crux pitch is appreciably harder than the rest of the route.

1.   140ft.   The lower section of the groove leads easily to below where the line steepens and deepens.

2.   130ft.   5a.   Continue up the back of the corner, rather a grovel in places, to a stance below a deep chimney. Bolt belays.

3.   85ft.   5a.   Climb the chimney. At its termination traverse left to gain the bottom of a corner, which leads to a stance on the left.

4.   85ft.   5c.   A steep wall on the right (pegs) gives difficult

climbing until the situation eases and a rightward rising traverse leads to a good ledge.

5.   100ft.   5a.   The all too obvious chimney gives a classic struggle to a small stance (peg belays).

6.   100ft.   4b.   The chimney continues, thankfully in a lighter vein to join the arête at a prominent tower.

DESCENT. Cross the ridge on to the south-west face, a short descent leads to abseil anchors. Two 80ft abseils (or one of 160ft) lead to a large tree. An 80ft abseil from this joins the descent route from VIA JULIA at the end of the ledge after the first abseil, continue down as for this descent.

DIEDRE MAGICS   ***   E2   640ft.

An excellent route giving sustained climbing up a fine line with the crux right at the top. Start about 200ft up to the right of the major groove line of VIA DIEDRE GALLEGO at a rather less conspicuous groove that slants up to the right.

1.   100ft.   5a.   Follow the shallow groove to a cave stance.

2.   80ft.   5a.   Continue in the same vein until the groove narrows and becomes a slanting crack.

3.   120ft.   5a.   The crack starts off amenably enough but gets harder as height is gained. Eventually things ease and a small stance is reached.

4.   140ft.   5a.   Continue up the obvious line with sustained interest (passing a possible stance at half height) to a belay on top of a pillar.

5.   100ft.   5b.   The pitch you have been waiting for. Climb the groove and swing smoothly over the roof (or make a total dog's dinner of it and grovel to safety). The ridge lies a short distance above.

DESCENT. 20ft right of the arrival point is an abseil anchor that allows the first of four long (120ft) abseils back to the base of the route. The end of the second abseil ends up on the stance above pitch three of the route. From here continue directly to the ground in two rope lengths.

DALLE D'OLA

Character

A compact wall of perfect rock equipped with plenty of big beefy (and brightly coloured) bolts. The cliff faces south-west from the lower slopes of Bernia, 3689ft (1128m) and affords magnificent views out over the coast. The tower blocks of the Black Hole of Benidorm can be seen glinting in the distance and beyond lie range upon range of unknown hills. The crag gets the sun from midday until it sets. A perfect spot to get the feel of Spanish rock.

For the rock hungry the southern slopes of Bernia, stretching away to the left of the crag, contain enough rock to last several lifetimes - but can you afford the bolts?

Approaches

From Calpe drive south on the N332 through the Mascarat gorge. Take the first right turn, signed Marina Greenwich ($1^1/2$ km after the gorge), or the much grander second right signed Altea Hills (2 km). Follow the road up over the motorway to a large flat area containing a complex junction/roundabout. Turn right and take a surfaced road which winds uphill. Eventually the road deteriorates into a gravel track; the crag is 400m down this. It is also possible to continue straight on at the complex junction and take a rough gravel road that approaches the cliff from the other direction. This is only recommended to the owners of four-wheel drive vehicles or donkeys. NOTE: there is considerable construction activity going on in this area, access details may change with time.

Descent

It is possible to climb down a rib to the left of the main section of the crag, but this is exposed and has one short steep section - care required. At the right side of the crag, 10ft below the edge and beside some blocks is a bolt/chain anchor which allows a 120ft abseil back

Jim Rubery on the Slabby Red Route (HVS 5a), Toix West

to base. Of course, any of the single bolt belays at the top of the routes can be used as abseil anchors, it is all a matter of confidence. How long are they anyway?

The routes do not have names as such but are known by their appropriate colour. Colour-blind climbers will have to seek help from their normal-sighted friends. Descriptions are from LEFT to RIGHT, and as all the climbs are 100-120ft in length this information has been omitted from the text.

To the left of the main wall of the crag and the slanting rake is a subsidiary buttress split by a red groove, the first two routes are found on this.

THE FAR LEFT YELLOW ROUTE * HVS 5a
Start to the left of the red corner at a flattened area. Climb up and left following a thin crack. As height is gained the crack steepens up and curves to the right. Bolts protect these steeper moves and a bolt belay is to be found on the rake.

The rock to the right of the red corner is taken by
THE LEFT YELLOW ROUTE * VS 4c
Follow either of the two bolt lines, the right-hand one being rather more difficult, to a belay on the sloping rake. Continue up the steeper wall above on good holds past two bolt runners to a bolt belay on top of the crag.

The rest of the climbs are on the main sheet of rock, the first four being reached by scrambling up to the left from the base of the crag.

THE BLACK ROUTE ** E2 5c
A rather unbalanced climb with the crux low down.

The steep lower wall is taken on small painful holds (almost a move of 6a) until below the bulge. A rest on the flakes on the left at this point is naughty (but nice). After passing the bulge with a long reach for a good jug the upper slab is an anticlimax. The bulge can also be

Graham Parkes cruising The Crack (E6 6b), Toix Sea Cliff

DALLE D'OLA

Abseil Point

Awkward
Descent

1. Left Yellow Route
2. Black Route
3. Pink Route
4. Green Route
5. Yellow Route
6. Silver Route
7. Blue Route
8. Pink Route
9. Red Route

crossed further to the right by another black bolt, but this is easier and even more of an anticlimax.

THE PINK ROUTE *** E1 5b
Sustained climbing and spaced bolts make this an entertaining pitch. Pull steeply on to the wall and climb boldly (in Spain?) leftwards to clip the first bolt. The bulging wall above is well furnished with jugs so press on to the second bolt. Once this is clipped relax and enjoy the rest of the route.

THE GREEN ROUTE *** E2 5c

A sustained pitch, perhaps the best on the cliff, with inspiring protection. Start at a large block.

Make difficult moves in a position of some safety to reach the first break. Continue steeply until the holds run out, a small side pull on a black "slug" to the left provides the key to gaining access to the interesting upper slab.

THE YELLOW ROUTE ** E1 5b

A good climb, quite stiff for the grade.

The lower section is the most difficult so clip in and press on. As the angle eases the bolts become more spaced and the climbing is much easier. Pass the upper bulge by the easy groove to its left.

THE SILVER ROUTE *** E2 5c

Another gem.

Steep fingery and sustained climbing with "bomber gear" leads to the slab. Saunter up this to the upper bulge which is taken at its left edge by a stiff pull. Once established over the roof step up and left to finish easily.

THE BLUE ROUTE ** E1 5b

A steady lower section leads to an awkward bulge at the top of the crag.

The lower wall has good holds and the slab above leads easily to the final bulge. This is taken centrally but unfortunately the expected jug does not materialise, so a little cunning is required to gain to the top.

THE PINK ROUTE ** E1 5b

Probably the easiest climb on the main section of the cliff, a good introduction.

The bolts are rather spaced on the lower wall but the holds are generally good. The slab above is interesting and should be tackled on the left. For those who are finding the whole experience a bit harrowing it is possible to trend right up easier rock directly to the abseil point.

THE RED ROUTE   **   E2   5b, 6a

A disjointed route with the upper pitch giving the hardest piece of climbing on the crag. A must for thugs.

Follow the right-hand line on the lower wall. This looks innocuous enough but has a couple of distinctly delicate moves. At the arrow walk right to a belay below the crack. The bolts above can be clipped by leaning in from the left, but are passed on the right by powerful undercutting and laybacking (with the odd jump) to reach the jugs above. A stout tree provides a suitable belay/lowering off point.

The opportunity exists for a multitude of rainbow-coloured girdles, the higher ones being of a more reasonable standard. Do them if you want but please don't report them.

Colin Binks on the Green Route (E2 5c), Dalle d'Ola

BARRANCO DEL MASCARAT

Just to the south of Calpe lies one of the major physical obstacles to north-south travel along the coastal plain, the combined ranges of the Sierra Bernia and Sierra de Toix. This almost continuous ridge of high limestone hills runs out into the sea to form a series of impressive cliffs. Cutting through this range of hills is the spectacular thousand-foot deep ravine of the Barranco del Mascarat. Crossing this magnificent feature are three impressive bridges, the lower two of which are the site of the now famous bridge jumping escapades. You are supposed to get a licence for this from the police in Alicante, but the majority of people don't bother. (Those with any sense don't bother with the jumping either.) See map p35.

Character
There is a wide variety of styles of climbing in this rather grim setting. In the base of the gorge are a series of one-pitch climbs; shady desperate test pieces on the south side contrast with slabby sunny much easier fare on the north side. At the level of the bridges are some short, hard climbs and the lower pitches of some longer "semi-alpine" routes.

Warning
By Sod's Law any material dropped off the upper pitches of the longer routes will land on the road, so either take great care or have adequate third party insurance.

Approach
The cliffs lie ten minutes drive southwards from Calpe on the N332. Parking is something of a problem, as cars left on the bridge are liable to be broken into, towed away, or both. If someone cannot be left with the car continue southwards and take the first surfaced left turn (1 km) signed Sol Ingrid, and Pueblo Mascarat. This leads back leftwards to a bridge crossing the dried-up stream bed issuing from the ravine, where there is a variety of parking spaces. The climbing is five

minutes rough walking from here.

The climbs at bridge level are described first.

LA TETA DE LA NOVIA   **   E3   500ft.

An interesting climb on good rock that takes the poorly defined buttress on the walls above the southern end of the central road tunnel. Reach the start by scrambling up from the downhill end of this tunnel. Cross the railway line and continue up a vague path in an open gully. This breaks out right past a small rock barrier. The start of the climb lies up and right and is marked by a cross and a pair of "door ornaments" scratched on the rock.

1.   120ft.   5c.   Follow the right-hand line of fixed gear up the front of the buttress to reach ledges below a bulge. Move left to climb a slippery flowstone wall protected by a couple of archaic bolts. Belay in the groove above.

2.   150ft.   5c.   Climb the groove until forced leftwards into another groove. Up this and the slabby wall above, where difficult moves right gain a crack (pegs) which leads to a stance.

3.   70ft.   5b.   Traverse right to a short awkward wall, up this (pegs) to a belay on the edge of the buttress.

4.   150ft.   5a.   Climb the corner system on the right to easy ground.

DESCENT. The summit of the mountain lies some distance above, only the most ardent of peak baggers will visit it. Otherwise follow a terrace to the left (southwards) and climb a 15ft wall (Diff) on to the open hillside. Turn left and descend eastwards into a gully then across the railway line to eventually reach the road. Do not be tempted to turn left too early on as there are cliffs below.

VIA U.P.S.A.   **   VS   790ft.

A long route through some impressive rock scenery. Unfortunately the crux pitch is rather out of character with the rest of the climbing. Start from the southern end of the old road bridge.

1.   120ft.   V.Diff rock leads past a variety of man-made objects to a peg belay on top of the first pillar.

23

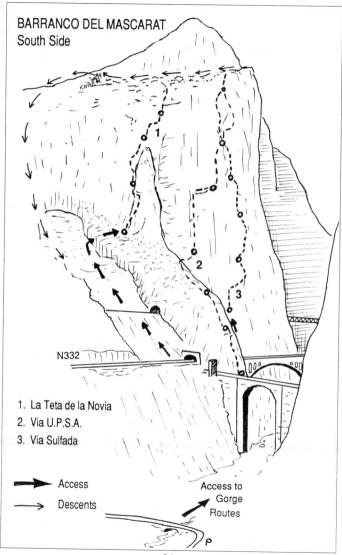

BARRANCO DEL MASCARAT
South Side

N332

1. La Teta de la Novia
2. Via U.P.S.A.
3. Via Sulfada

➤ Access

→ Descents

Access to
Gorge
Routes

24

2.   120ft.   3c.   A short awkward wall leads to easier rock and a belay where the angle falls back.

3.   150ft.   Easy climbing up the crest of the ridge leads to vegetated terraces that are followed leftwards until it is possible to move right to below a groove in the more impressive upper section of the route.

4.   100ft.   3c.   Climb up into the groove then make a couple of moves right before climbing straight up the wall to ledges. A traverse is then made to a stance on the right.

5.   120ft.   4c.   Above and right lurks the crux groove. This is gained and followed by sustained moves (or pulling on the pegs if you are an alpinist) until easier climbing leads to a stance on the right.

6.   80ft.   4a.   Step left and climb straight up to a good thread from which a rising traverse to the right leads to a stance with bolt belays.

7.   100ft.   4b.   Move up to a peg in a diagonal crack then swing right around the arête to gain a corner which eases as height is gained and leads to a shoulder above all difficulties.

DESCENT. Regain the mountain by traversing the narrow ridge (a stroll for the confident, an 'à cheval' grovel for the more timid). Peak baggers can continue up the ridge for a couple of hundred feet of V.Diff climbing on good rock to reach the summit of the Mascarat Superior followed by a descent to the south. Ordinary mortals, especially those with sore feet, can follow the terrace to the left to join the descent of the previous route.

VIA SULFADA   ***   E1   730ft.
An excellent outing on superb rock in a dramatic setting. Start at the uphill end of the middle road tunnel. The first two easy pitches can be soloed but the scenario in the event of a slip is all too obvious.

1.   80ft.   Climb over the railings then up to the right over vegetated rock to a ledge. Follow the easy groove above past a thin thread until the line leads left to a ledge and two bolt belay.

2.   90ft.   Step right then plough up the herbal gully (thread) before moving right to a peg and thread belay below a groove in steeper rock. Things now begin to improve.

3. 120ft. 5b. Climb the groove to two bolts, which are passed by steep bridging. Step right then continue in the same line past pegs and bolts to enter a groove. Up this to an exit left then climb diagonally left to a small stance and three bolt belay. The downward views are most photogenic.

4. 100ft. 5b. Step right then climb straight up for 30ft. Now traverse to the right to enter a hidden groove which is followed past several pegs (some of which stick out rather a long way) to another excellent stance.

5. 80ft. 5b. Up the steep wall behind the stance to gain access to a slabby groove. Up this to its end then straight up the crack above until a traverse left brings you to another fine stance.

6. 150ft. 5a. Climb the red corner behind the belay, it contains no fixed gear so a couple of large Rocks are useful. At its top step left on to some large flakes (peg) then follow easier cracks to a comfy ledge.

7. 150ft. 5a. It is possible to finish up the top pitch of the previous route (4b). Alternatively trend left into a groove which is followed until it steepens, then either cop out by traversing left, or climb the strenuous jamming crack past the bush (runners required) to the top.

DESCENT is as for the previous route.

The next routes described are reached by crossing the old road bridge. The wall to the right of the tunnel door contains some man-made finger pockets. Prospective suitors of CLEOPLACA should spend some time hanging off these to get warmed up (if you need to use the footholds you are in for a hard time).

Scramble up left to a ledge with two bolts. The small tunnel to the left is worth a visit by those with an exploratory bent to their nature

The obvious slanting groove containing several pegs is pitch 3 of AURORA, which starts from the gorge bed. The wall to the right of the groove is the site of three fine climbs reached by scrambling carefully up quarried rock past cacti (a very un-British hazard). The wall gets the sun after midday.

CLEOPLACA *** E6 6b 155ft.
A magnificent pitch taking the centre of the stunning diamond-shaped brown wall. Start at a single bolt belay just to the right of the slabby groove. The initial wall gives a taste of things to come and is climbed first left then back right. Above this an easier section leads past a huge 'ringing' flake. The upper wall is sustained and the route finding is intricate with only just enough bolt protection and little in the way of rests. Peg and bolt belay/abseil anchor.

AGUJA INFERIOR ** E2 180ft.
A good climb in a spooky setting, though overshadowed by its immediate neighbours. Begin below a weakness with a peg in it to the right of the bolt belay of CLEOPLACA.
1. 100ft. 5b. A couple of tricky moves are needed to get started, thread. Improving holds lead up onto a ramp which is followed up to the right past good but spaced peg runners. A final difficult few moves (hint - stay low) lead to a well endowed stance.
2. 80ft. 5b. The slanting groove is followed past bolts and pegs and gives sustained climbing until the bolt belay on CLEO-PLACA is reached. The route continues for some distance but the climbing does not compare with that below so a 150ft abseil back to safety is the best idea.

BRIDGE OF SPIES *** E6 6c 80ft.
A route that is all it appears, taking a feature almost as impressive as the prow of the QE2. Start at the top of the gully on the right side of the wall below a bolt ladder running up to the first stance on AGUJA INFERIOR. (Possibly E5 6b but no details available.) The route takes the grossly leaning prow to the right of this line.
    Follow the bolts to gain a large black 'caterpillar' containing two threads. Climb this (it requires a most unusual technique) and then make desperate moves up and right to gain a flake hidden from below. Easier climbing now leads to twin bolts. Lower off and go for a beer, you deserve it.

SPINACH PLEASE OLIVE E4 6c 30ft.
A well named route to delight the connoisseurs of the trivial. Takes

the wall just to the right of the tunnel entrance with two bolt runners and a hideous move using the obvious "mono doigt." Just remember tendons have feelings too.

To the right is a concaved wall with two short routes. No details known.

The rest of the routes start from the bed of the gorge, reached either by walking up the stream bed, see Approaches, or by a 150ft abseil from the paired bolts below CLEOPLACA.

The base of the gorge is an interesting but sinister spot with traffic thundering by far above. Scattered around are huge boulders brought down by flash floods and the remnants of many safes brought from who knows where. It is worth a short walk upstream to where the walls close in and the atmosphere is even more impressive (or should it be oppressive), certainly not a place to be when it rains!

The routes are described on the north side of the gorge first, starting with a climb that reascends the line of the abseil and then weaves its way up the buttress above.

AURORA ** E2 720ft.
A long route which takes a devious line and visits some interesting spots.
Start between the two road bridges at an attractive light-coloured slab with a well trodden area at its base.
1.   120ft. 5b.   Climb leftwards into the centre of the wall and then head straight on up (easier variations to the left are vastly inferior). At 80ft a couple of trickier moves up a flake lead to easier rock and a little higher is a small stance and peg belay on the right.
2.   40ft. 5b.   Move left to below a shallow groove which is entered from the left by a piggish move. A short distance above is the terrace and an escape for those who have had enough. The next objective is the slanting groove above. Do not try to get at it from below (dangerously loose) but move right and up to the bolt belay below CLEOPLACA.
3.   100ft. 5b.   Step into the groove and follow it delicately to

steeper moves on better holds. Pass a perfect bivi site to an exposed stance on the left.

4.   70ft.   5b.   Gain the well-pegged crack directly or more easily from the left, and follow it with sustained interest until it becomes possible to swing right onto easier rock. A small stance lies a short distance above.

5.   110ft.   4c.   Cross the slab on the left to its far corner, then climb diagonally across the steep left wall to gain access to easy rock. Traverse easily leftwards until a belay can be taken below a massive red corner with a prominent bolt in its left wall.

6.   110ft.   5a.   The corner is steep and imposing but it is less difficult than appearances might suggest. The mean looking wide crack in the upper section is outflanked on the left, and a slab leads to a stance.

7.   100ft.   4a.   The easy slab on the left is crossed and the corner above is entered past a "pothole." The giant flakes are climbed most easily and safely on the left and lead to a comfortable grass ledge.

8.   70ft.   4c.   The steep crack on the right is awkward to enter, but once gained leads more easily to a rather sudden finish.

DESCENT. Follow the rocky ridge northwards until it runs out into open hillside. Continue up to the ruin on the summit, from where a rough track leads north-east to the villas below Toix West.

The next climbs are a series of short bolt-protected pitches which lie to the right (south-west) of the old road bridge on a steep grey wall which contains a prominent vertical cave to the right of the smoothest section.

BLACK ORCHID   **   E2   5c   80ft.
Begin below and left of the cave entrance. Climb up to the right until it is possible to pull left to the first bolt. The crux lies just above and involves strenuous use of an undercut pocket. A few more steep moves lead on to a slab which is climbed to the left of the bolts to a belay/lowering point.

AUNTY BOLT   **   E2   5c   80ft.
Slightly easier than its companion. Climb up into the cave (optional thread on the left- not in situ) and bridge up to the first bolt. The steep wall has a selection of good holds but is strenuous, until the angle eases. Climb the slab keeping to the right of some rather familiar bolts to the belay.

SOFT ROCK   *   E1   5b   155ft.
A route that takes a line to the right of the cave and which improves as height is gained.
   Head up to the right by some surprisingly awkward moves until it is possible to climb straight up passing some man-sized threads. The smart grey slab above leads to a single bolt belay. Abseil off this or walk to the left to the twin bolts below CLEOPLACA.

A few paces to the right is a short grey slab that has two slight but pleasant fillers-in.

BROTHER WOLF   HVS   5a   60ft.
The left-hand line climbs up a groove and over a bulge passing a substantial thread. Above this trend slightly right to a lowering bolt.

SISTER MOON   HVS   5a   60ft.
Start to the right at the lowest point of the wall and take a direct line, (or weave about a bit if you want) to the abseil anchor.

The final routes described in the gorge are on the impressive leaning wall peppered with pockets that lies almost directly below the new road bridge. The wall is in the sun for a couple of hours around midday, at other times it can provide a welcome shady retreat. The names of the climbs are painted very elegantly on the rock. All the pitches can be done to the belays and back to the ground on a 165ft (50m) rope though they feel much, much bigger.

Chris Craggs on the crux of Black Orchid (E2 5c), Mascarat Gorge

EL SHERRIFICO   ***   E6   6b   90ft.

At the left side of the wall is a line of closely spaced bolts shooting skywards. These are the starting point of a brilliant and butch pitch.

The line of bolts is followed up the leaning wall using a variety of painful finger pockets and slippery footholds until jugs are reached. Move up and right on better holds then back left to below the more impressive upper section. The holds are mostly good but the angle approaches the ludicrous until a few final difficult moves gain the slab above and twin lowering bolts. A mean dude.

HAMBRE DE MUJER   ***   E4   6a   90ft.

The easiest of the bunch but another tough cookie, taking the shallow sinuous groove up the middle of the wall.

Begin in the centre of the wall from the left-most of a series of blocks. A steep starts leads to better but spaced holds which are followed up and right to a large hole (threads). Continue leftwards up the slightly easier angled wall until the groove steepens up and some harrowing bridging is required to reach the sanctuary of a cave. It is possible to hide a while in here but glory lies only a short distance away around to the left. Don't worry about falling off - you won't hit anything.

QUE DIOS REPARTE SUERTE   **   E6   6c   90ft.

A mighty pitch up the smoothest part of the wall, well protected but with a desperate starting sequence. Fierce moves on pinch grips, pockets and the odd chopped dink lead up the leaning lower wall (with luck and a pinch of talent) to the easier angled 'slab' above. Those who have flashed this section might as well bale off from the large bolt as they may find the upper section something of a disappointment. Normal mortals should enjoy this section which gives quality pocket climbing until a belay on the slab above can be reached.

Chris Craggs in the setting sun on El Dorado (E2 5b),Toix Sea Cliffs

LUBRICANTE VAGINAL EN UNO * E4 6b 40ft.

A delightfully named piece of climbing that takes the obscenely angled wall to the right followed by the butch layback above. Start below and left of the base of the flake crack at a rightward rising line of bolts. A couple of desperate moves (or a large cairn, E3 5c) using the feature the route is named after, lead to the first decent pocket. The rest of the route is just plain hard work - follow the bolts strenuously to the base of the flake. Continue up this until it is possible to swing right to a lowering bolt.

The final route in this area lies 100m further into the dragons lair where the walls close in and a slabby rib on the left gives a way through the initial barrier of overhangs.

ABDUL *** E6 6b 80ft.

A route with an impact considerably greater than its length might suggest.

Climb the slabby rib then move slightly right to reach a pockety crack leading leftwards. From the end of this a swine of a move gains the slab on the left and a rest (you are going to need it). When suitably recovered swing around the undercut corner on to a leaning pocketed wall which is climbed leftwards to another difficult exit on to another slab. The final obstacle is the 12ft roof with the belays dangling tantalisingly from the lip, go for it.

High on the wall opposite ABDUL is an obvious but inaccessible bolt protected layback crack. No details are known.

Dave Spence on the crux of El Oso y El Madrono (E2 5c), Toix East

SIERRA DE TOIX

The Sierra de Toix is the long rocky ridge that runs eastwards from the gorge of the Barranco del Mascarat, to disappear into the sea as the rocky headland of Toix East. The northern side of the ridge is the site of the Maryvilla complex, a sprawl of impressive white-walled villas that are scattered over almost every available piece of land, irrespective of angle.

Character
Four cliffs are described, with Toix East and West offering short open and well protected routes that are easy of access and often of a reasonable grade on perfect but rough rock. The Toix Sea Cliff/South are rather more serious and a little tricky of access, but they are well worth the effort. Toix North is a shady retreat from the searing sun, it contains some short sharp pitches by the road and some sterner stuff on the upper crag. Climbs can be enjoyed in the sun at any time of the day with just a little forethought. Access is described separately for each cliff.

Toix Sea Cliff / South Face

A large impressive crag that rises as the name suggests straight from the sea. Some of the rock is a rather strange red/brown colour and looks dangerously loose, but it is mostly well cemented and the cliff gives some of the most impressive pitches in this guide. In atmosphere and angle it is somewhat similar to the 'gentleman's side' of Huntsman's Leap.

The Sea Cliff is in the sun from shortly after midday until sunset, it is a beautiful place to spend the evening.

SIERRA DE TOIX and BARRANCO DEL MASCARAT
Layout

CLIFFS

1. Mascarat Gorge
2. Toix Sea Cliff
3. Toix West
4. Toix North
5. Toix East

Access

There are two ways of getting to the boulder beach that allows access to the left end of the crag. Firstly, it is possible to walk from the parking place below Toix West by following the track down the hillside. As this peters out head to the right (facing the sea) across old quarried terraces until rough scrambling leads to the beach.

Secondly and more easily, drive south on the N332 through the tunnels of the Mascarat Gorge and take the first surfaced left turn, signed Sol Ingrid and Pueblo Mascarat (1 km from the tunnels). Follow the road down the hill and over a dried up stream bed to a junction. Turn left and park on the left after a couple of hundred metres. There is a lot of development going on in this area at the time of writing and it is something of a cross between a building site and a bomb site. Because of this access arrangements may change. From the parking place cross the "boulder field" and follow a rough track down across old terraces to the boulder beach.

Descent

Most of the climbs finish on the conspicuous slanting rake that runs across the top of the crag. This can be followed up to the left to escape onto easy ground above the crag, but this is exposed and a little loose - not recommended. It is also possible to climb straight up from several points on the terrace to reach the top of the crag (easy but no fixed gear). The best and safest option is to abseil back to the beach from the rake. Almost directly above the beach is a bunch of threads on the rake; a 100ft abseil from these leads over an overhang to the end of a ledge. Move left (looking in) to more anchors that allow a 140ft abseil back to the beach.

THE CRACK *** E6 270ft.

A superb thin crack forms the main substance of this route though it is unfortunately hacked around. Somebody has 'created' a masterpiece (or is it a monster).

1.   100ft.   4b.   From the beach traverse to the right a short distance above the water to a rounded crack. Go up this then continue the traverse to gain a good ledge and triple bolt belay.

2.   100ft.   6b.   To the left of the stance a thin crack soars up the

wall. This gives superb sustained finger jamming and laybacking on near frictionless rock with spaced bolt protection, several small rocks and R.P.s will be needed by all but the bold. Eventually it is possible to swing left on better holds where the rock starts to bulge and strenuous jug pulling leads eventually to a semi-hanging two bolt belay.

3.　70ft.　5c.　Continue directly up the steep wall and onto the slab above. This leads to the rake a short distance below the abseil point.

Directly above the stance at the end of pitch one is a smooth leaning wall with a line of bolts up it. It looks desperate but no details are known.

EL DORADO I　***　E2　280ft.
A magnificent intimidating line, strenuous but well protected up the red chimney crack in the centre of the face.

1.　100ft.　4b.　As for pitch one of THE CRACK to the triple bolt belay.

2.　100ft.　5b.　Climb up to the right to reach the first bolt which is passed awkwardly on the right by steep moves to gain a niche in the base of the chimney proper. The overhanging section above is bridged with ample protection from bolts and threads until a few strenuous pulls on good but "funny" holds lead to a gripping hanging stance on two large threads and a couple of pegs.

3.　80ft.　5b.　From the stance climb steeply leftwards on sloping holds to a peg and slightly higher, an obvious thread. Now climb up the centre of the fine grey slab above, a great contrast to the butch goings on below. All too soon a bolt, peg and thread belay are reached on the rake.

EL DORADO II　**　E3　260ft.
The bulging wall to the right of the chimney crack of EL DORADO I gives a strenuous piece of climbing, with good protection and good but often spaced holds.

1.　100ft.　4b.　As for pitch one of THE CRACK to the three bolt stance. If this is crowded it is possible to belay 30ft further to the right directly below the line at the end of a fixed rope that runs out to the arête.

2.   100ft.   5c.   From the start of the fixed rope climb up the steep wall bearing slightly to the left, until close to EL DORADO I. From here the line leads to the right to a hanging stance below a line of bulges.

3.   60ft.   5b.   The obvious line leading steeply rightwards leads strenuously to the rake.

A similar looking line but with a smooth central section starts in the same place and eventually veers to the right but no details are available.

VIA MISSING LINK   ***   E3   370ft.   *En 31 Dec '92*

The impressive arête of the crag gives an atmospheric pitch with a long approach. A superb expedition. Carry a few medium nuts and Friends. Parties who are experiencing difficulty on the route can traverse right after 40ft to gain a cave belay. From here climb up and right to eventually gain the terrace. The overall grade of this variation is E2 (5c) and it is known as LUCES NOCTURNAS.

1.   100ft.   4b.   As for pitch one of THE CRACK to the three bolt stance.

2.   120ft.   5b.   Descend the flake crack to the right of the belay until just above the water line (peg) then traverse easily on good holds but without much protections until things get a little tougher. Awkward moves up to the right lead to a descending line of jugs which are followed to a hanging stance on two rusty bolts. A fall from this pitch by leader or second may not prove fatal but will certainly dampen their enthusiasm for the rest of the route.

The fixed rope at the stance is useful for keeping the climbing ropes out of the water and provides an escape route if problems arise.

3.   150ft.   5b. if you are strong, 5c is you are not.

Climb the slabby wall above the stance to steeper rock and some insubstantial threads. Continue up a flake crack just to the right of the arête until it is possible to pull back leftwards onto the prow (a cave stance is available 30ft right at this point but it is vastly more satisfying to run out the arête in one pitch). Now follow a line to the right of the arête (threads) into the final groove which is bridged to the rake. A superb pitch but don't look down.

From the stance on the rake it is possible to climb the crack above (severe) or traverse to the left up the rake to get back to the beach as described under DESCENT. A third option is to descend the narrow rake (keeping the rope on) to the right for 100ft to a bolt belay at the foot of a wall which is taken by LE GALLEON, E2 5c, thus giving an excellent five or six pitch tour of the crag.

Toix South is the kilometre of rock that runs from the great arête of MISSING LINK to Toix East. It bears a resemblance to Great Zawn on the Little Orme but unlike its Welsh counterpart this crag gets the sun all day. Much of it is undercut at the base and development is still in its infancy.

The top of the cliff is most easily reached by walking down the track from the parking place below Toix West. Access to the routes is by abseil from above where the names and the length of rope required are painted on the rock. Unfortunately the grades are not included in this information so a little caution is sensible unless you are after an adventure.

The only route described is reached by a 120ft abseil from a point about 100ft to the left of the arête (looking out to sea) using anchors in a slab just below the cliff edge. Look for the name on the rock.

✓ LE GALLEON ** E2 5c 120ft. *2nd* .

Climb straight back up the grey wall on exceptionally rough rock following the line of bolts and threads and the occasional chiselled hold to a horizontal break. Continue up easier angled smoother rock avoiding easier ground on both sides. It is possible to split the pitch at half-height on a large flake to the right, bolt and large thread belay.

Toix West

Character

An easily accessible crag that provides an excellent selection of short routes with a few longer ones for good measure. The left side of the cliff provides steeper pitches while around to the right the angle is rather more amenable. The rock is perfect and bolts abound. The right side of the crag gets the sun from midday whereas the left side is only in the sun in the evening, so you can get scorched or climb in the shade according to personal preference and weather conditions. The majority of the climbs have no names but are recognised by the colour of the bolts. This makes for easy route recognition but boring pub talk.

Access (see Map Page 35)

The cliff is reached from the Maryvilla Complex which is at the southern end of the bay at Calpe. From Calpe go out on to the N332 and head south towards Alicante for about 1 km. Just as the road begins to descend into the Mascarat Gorge, at a right-hand bend turn left into the villa complex (signed Urbanisacion Maryvilla). The junction is also recognisable by the giant Michelin man on the hillside above it. Coming from the south it is the first right turn after the Mascarat Gorge, situated where the road begins to flatten out. It is easy to overshoot the junction from this direction.

Once in the complex take the first three right turns. The narrow road leads steeply uphill and over a brow to an adequate parking space at the end of the tarmac. The cliff is two minutes away.

The routes are described from LEFT to RIGHT. Descents are described after each route.

THE YELLOW ROUTE   **   VS   330ft.

A long and interesting climb that leads to the top of the cliff though it can be abandoned at several points en route. Start at the left edge of the cliff.

1.   80ft.   4a.   Climb the steep lower section to easier angled rock that is taken left then right to a good ledge and belay.

40

2.   80ft.   4c.   The steep wall behind the stance is taken direct on (mostly) good holds to a ledge and single bolt belay. The crux over and done with, the ground can be reached by a 150ft abseil, but true mountaineers will want to press on.

3.   70ft.   4a.   Move out to the left to find the easiest line which is followed up and then back to the right to another excellent stance. A more direct version of the pitch is HVS 5a.

4.   100ft.   Follow the crest of the ridge easily to the top.

DESCENT. Either abseil 150ft down the north side of the ridge, and if you land in somebody's garden explain that you are English and lost. Alternatively, follow the crest of the ridge to the east until easy scrambling leads down to the right (south) and back below the cliff.

The next three routes take the walls of the steep bowl that form the left side of the main cliff.

THE SILVER ROUTE   *   E1   150ft.
A rather devious route but it takes the easiest line up a steep piece of rock.
Start in the back left corner of the bay below a niche.

1.   70ft.   5c.   Make a couple of steep moves in to the niche and pull quickly out rightward (crux). Follow steep rock up to the left past bolts and a peg over a small roof, avoiding the easy corner on the left. At a tree move right to a small stance and multibolt belay.

2.   80ft.   5b.   Move right to gain the conspicuous leftward leaning corner which is followed awkwardly to an easy groove that leads to a good stance and single bolt belay.

DESCENT. Either abseil 150ft directly to the ground from the belay, or more safely traverse 40ft to the right to the tree and belays above THE RED ROUTE from where a 150ft abseil leads back to the ground.

THE GREEN ROUTE   **   E2   150ft.
Two excellent steep pitches with "bomber gear" allowing the experience to be enjoyed to the full.
Start at a short rightward rising ramp in the back of the bay.

1.   70ft.   5c.   From the top of the ramp swing awkwardly up to

the left to gain a series of flakes that rise to the right. These lead steeply to a semi-rest at a break. Pull rightwards onto the steep wall and follow improving holds to below a bulge. Despite appearances to the contrary good holds do exist on the wall above allowing a swing left to be made to the stance on the SILVER ROUTE.

2.   80ft.   5c.   Step right and attack the steep wall above. A difficult swing left on tiny holds allows access to good flakes that are followed to the steep but easy groove above. This leads to a large stance and bolt belay.

DESCENT. As for the SILVER ROUTE.

At the time of writing no route exists up the steepest part of the back wall of the bay, though it does sprout a solitary bolt. Fame and fortune await the man with the Bosch.

THE RED ROUTE   ***   E2   5c   160ft.
A magnificent varied pitch up the right edge of the bay. Quite hard for the grade but with exemplary protection; 15 quick draws should suffice but watch the rope drag.
Start at the right toe of the bay at a 20ft high pillar just right of two large fallen flakes.

Climb the pillar to the first bolt, difficult moves into and out of the niche above may be the crux for many, especially 'shorthausens.' A steep flake above leads to a thin move where the angle eases. The style of climbing now changes. Teeter up the ramp to the left until all appears lost. A jug three feet to the left is the key: climb, jump or fall across to it. Now head up to the right crossing the "blank" slab on a well-hidden jug to easier but steep climbing. A good ledge above has a bolt and thread belay.

DESCENT. A 150ft abseil from the belays or from the tree to the right leads back to the ground.

THE BLACK ROUTE   **   E3   6a   160ft.

A good route rather spoilt by the out-of-character nature of the crux section. This can be avoided by the groove to its right which makes the overall grade a more balanced E2 5c. Start as for the RED ROUTE.

Climb the pillar as for the RED ROUTE, then continue slightly rightwards up the steep wall to an easier angled section. Step left onto the smooth face and make fingery and committing moves up and left to a bolt. Step back to the right then climb straight up easier angled rock, passing a loose hold which has fallen off, with difficulty. Continue in a direct line via more thin moves to pass to the right of a big detached block to arrive at the tree and belay of the RED ROUTE. Descend as for the RED ROUTE.

ANOTHER GREEN ROUTE   **   HVS   5a   150ft.

An excellent pitch recently equipped with new bolts but still containing some interesting relics of the Iron Age. Start at a rounded groove just to the right of the pillar at the start of the RED and BLACK routes.

Climb the right side of the groove and the thin crack above to reach the base of a superb slab. Up this to its apex then follow the diagonal crack to its top. (Possible belay to the right.) Make a difficult move onto the wall then trend right to the huge flake system up which the route finishes. The difficult wall can be avoided by climbing the wide crack, containing two large wedges, further to the right.

DESCENT is by a 150ft abseil from a bolt and large thread.

The next routes lie at the lowest point of the crag where the rock is much more slabby.

THE SLABBY RED ROUTE   *   HVS   170ft.

An interesting lower pitch leads to easier exposed climbing above. Start at the bottom of the slab at a line of red spots, hoping they are not contagious.

1.   70ft.   5a.   Follow the line as closely as possible, it is rather easier to the right of the bolts, passing the occasional "red herring" to a juggy bulge and a good stance (R1).

2.   100ft.   4c.   Step left and plod up the open corner to a large detached flake. Step gingerly over this and move left into a bulging corner which leads to easy ground. The abseil point for the RED and BLACK ROUTES lies 30ft to the left. Use it.

THE BLUE ROUTE   *   HVS   170ft.
Rather tougher than its near neighbours.
1.   70ft.   5b.   Straight up the slabby wall following the appropriate colour coded bolts over a bulge to a stance slightly above that of the previous route.
2.   100ft.   5a.   Above lies a bulging corner crack whose bark is worse than its bite. Romp up this to a swing round the final obstacle to easy ledges.

The DESCENT is as for the previous route.

★ ★ better than CG suggests

DIRE STRAITS   *   HVS   5b   70ft. ✓ *Led Dee '92*
Distinguished from the other routes in this area by having a name, but not by much else. The start is rather obvious.
Climb up to the right to pass the bonsai tree. The steep section above is easier than it looks, just tear up the dotted line. Traverse left to the belay of the previous route. Abseil from here or continue up the BLUE ROUTE.

The next climbs described lie around to the right and up the bank slightly in a bowl, a real sun trap.

THE RIGHT-HAND RED ROUTE   *   E1   5b   70ft.
This route climbs a thin crack in a rib and gives pleasant if somewhat brief exercise. Start below the crack. Gain the crack via a couple of thin moves (or by the indirect start just to the right, 5c) and follow it past several peg runners with surprising difficulty, until the rib on the right can be gained. This leads easily to a lowering point.

The final of climbs in this area are in the back of the bowl-shaped area.

Colin Binks on The Right-hand Red Route (E1 5c), Toix West

John Evans.

THE GREEN ROUTE ** E1 150ft. *Mon 28 Dec '92*

Start at a pedestal/flake below a groove. A pleasantly delicate exercise, with a rather poorly protected left-hand top pitch (carry a few middle to large rocks).

1. 80ft. 5b. From the top of the pedestal climb thinly right-wards to get into the groove. Continue past several pegs to gain and follow a crack which leads to the stance in a small niche, peg and bolt belay.

2. 70ft Either (5a) in contrast to the pitch below, climb the chimney groove above the stance (pegs) to a bolt belay,

    or, (5b) in keeping with the pitch below, move left and climb the delicate face to reach the same stance.

DESCENT. A 150ft abseil from the belay will take you back to the ground.

EL MENU DE DIA * E2 6a or HVS 5a 150ft.

Slabby climbing on perfect rock with an element of choice.

Start at a deep rounded groove with a line of pale pink (very twee) bolts. Follow the groove until it steepens and things begin to look rather grim (at the last chain link bolt). Holidaymakers and those in search of an easy time should move right into a groove which is followed back left. Hot shots should continue left and make thin moves to a finger jug before swinging back right to regain the previous variation. From the meeting of the ways easier climbing leads up the rib to a good stance on the left reached by a short traverse.

DESCENT. A 140ft abseil, or an awkward scramble up and then down to the right. The former is preferable except for those who suffer from fear of heights.

THE BLACK ROUTE ** VS 4b 140ft.

A rather sombre colour for a very pleasant pitch.

Start up the slabby rib to the right of the bowl. Easy angled climbing past a possible stance at 40ft leads up the crest of the ridge into a corner until a traverse leads left to the belay and a descent as for the previous climb.

Some distance up the hillside to the right of the main crag is a conspicuous grey slab of perfect rock reached by an arduous ten minute scramble. It contains two short routes that are worth seeking out if the main crag is crowded.

LEFT LINE   E2   5c   60ft.   *Led   Dec '92*

Climb up to the prominent bolt in the centre of the slab and pass it with difficulty. Continue in the same line to another bolt and a little higher a lowering station.

RIGHT LINE   HVS   5a   60ft.   *2nd Dec '92.*

Follow a curving undercut flake up to the right to the bolt on its lip. Keep heading in the same direction to gain a slanting crack that leads back to the left (threads) to a belay.

Still further up the hill is a steep sided, south facing bowl of red rock. It can be a real furnace in the middle of the day and is perhaps best visited in the evening. It can be reached from Toix West in about 15 minutes via the gully and scrubby slopes to its right. Alternately and somewhat more pleasantly follow the directions to Toix West to the third junction. Keep left and follow the road to a fork. The right branch leads out to the headland (superb views) and then round to a small parking space by the antennae on top of the hill. The crag is just out of site five minutes scramble away over rough ground. It contains at least three impressive routes.

The left-hand line is a three pitch 'super route:' a wall, a groove and a mighty impressive roof. Judging by appearances it must have more E numbers than a Pot Noodle.

The right-hand line is a blank looking wall which is bound to have more holds than can be seen from the bottom (i.e. none).

The central line has a rather trivial first pitch and a fine second one although it is rather dwarfed by its neighbour to the left. This is:

CENTRAL WALL   **   E5   160ft.

Start in a dusty cave in the back of the bay.

1.   60ft.   6a.   Bridge up the back of the hollow to a thread then swing right to a couple of bolts. Make one difficult pull on spiky holds

to gain the rugged slab, amble up this to a thread and bolt belay.

2.   100ft.   6a.   Step right and pull back left in to a hollow. Now climb steeply up and then right using a blatant chiselled hold to reach a flowstone pillar. Move up and right on a horn and cross the bulge on spaced finger jugs. Easier climbing leads to the final steep crack which gives a couple of powerful moves past a good thread. Belay on blocks well back.

DESCENT. Scramble down the ridge until it is possible to break out to the right back to the gear.

The view down from P.9 Via Gomez Cano (E2 5c), Penon de Ifach
Colin Binks on Balinulus Guttulatus (E4 6b), Gandia

Toix North

Character

A crag that is in the shade for most of the day and as such can prove useful 'when the heat is on.' Those who want to do these routes while they are in the sun will have to get up early in the morning. The climbs on the lower cliff are short and on rough rock, they are all very well protected and have lowering bolts, wire cables and karabiners in place. The routes on the upper cliff are longer and on rather smoother rock and the bolts are sometimes a bit spaced. They can be done to the belays and back to the ground on a 165ft rope, but only just.

Access (see Map Page 35)

The routes are to be found on and near the conspicuous large white wall at the right end of the long line of rock that fringes the upper edge of the whole of the north side of the Sierra de Toix. An unfinished villa on stilts is also a landmark. From the entrance to the Maryvilla Complex (as for Toix West) take the first two right turns and bear left at the third junction. The road is followed past a right turn to a fork. Follow the right branch and take the next right turn. The road contours back along the hillside and then bends sharply back to the left before ending by the previously mentioned villa. There is room to turn and park here. The lower crag is the bulging red wall you have just driven past, the upper crag is the big white face above and is reached in two minutes by a small diagonal path.

The lower crag is described first, from LEFT to RIGHT.

Warning! Along the foot of the crag runs a rather wobbly water pipe that supplies the villas below. Unfortunately all of the routes use it to get started; please treat it gently.

LA NINA   E3   6a   30ft.
Starting to the left of the undercut base of the crag pass the first bolt by some difficult moves to reach a diagonal crack. Using finger jams in this, rock out right to reach much easier climbing and the 'hook.'

LA NOVIA   E3   6a   30ft.
Start directly below the belay bolts. Climb into a depression and exit from it slightly rightwards using a good but discrete sidepull. A couple more tricky moves lead to the anchor.

LA VIULA   E2   6a   30ft.
The right-hand line has an awkward undercut start requiring a short, sharp pull on short, sharp holds. The scoop above, past a thread, is trivial by comparison.

PINON   *   E4   6b   45ft.
This route starts by ascending to the prominent large hole, lean left from this and launch onto the wall. Good but spaced holds lead to the last protection bolt, from here levitate to the belay.

The other two routes on the lower crag are found a short distance down the road to the right at an undercut scoop that has a back wall covered in flowstone.

RIGHT ROUTE LEFT   *   E4   6a   70ft.
Start at the left side of the scoop and pull rightwards over the bulge. Continue with difficulty past a big bolt to reach a hole then follow a wiggly crack to much better holds at the break. When rested, attack the upper bulges on holds that bear a striking resemblance to an amalgam of broken glass and razor blades. For those with thick skin the belay is not far away!

RIGHT ROUTE RIGHT   *   E4   6a   70ft.
The right-hand line of bolts is followed on good but spaced jugs until a difficult move up a scoop (passing a missing hold) leads to the break. The upper section is taken leftwards to the lowering bolts.

The upper crag contains three routes of which two are described here. The left-most line is POR QUIEN DOBLON LAS ESQUINES, a steep pitch that trends slightly rightwards up the wall and looks to be in the E5/6 category.

CENTRAL WALL   ***   E5   6b   90ft.
The formidable central line on the wall keeping to the left of the brown streaked groove. Climb to the tip of a pointed flake to reach the first bolt, then climb steep flaky rock past one or two suspicious finger jugs to a black hole (don't get sucked in). Continue with more difficulty to a wooden hand hold then make the crux moves before trending slightly left then back right to jugs. A final few reachy moves to the left gains the lowering bolts.

NOTE. The ground is slightly more than half a rope length away, so don't loose the end of the rope.

S.S.   ***   E5   6a   80ft.
An excellent pitch that takes the pockety seam to the right of the central brown groove line (which bears a striking resemblance to Original Route at High Tor and is unclimbed at present).

Gain the bulge at the bottom of the seam by climbing past a prominent peg (a Charlet Moser Universal to the uninitiated). A couple of fierce pulls on sharp pockets gain better holds, which are followed by repeating the same move several times until a resting place is reached. At this point it may look like your right arm belongs to Popeye and your left one to Olive Oil. Easier rock now leads to the lowering point.

Toix East

Character

A very popular and easily accessible crag, (these two facts may not be totally unrelated) with a good selection of short climbs across a broad range of difficulty. The routes are invariably well protected by chain link bolts, and apart from quick draws the only equipment worth carrying is one or two slings to replace missing threads. The rock is very rough and a sustained period of climbing here requires either skin like a rhino or a high resistance to pain.

The crag gets the sun from dawn until a couple of hours after midday and it can be at its most pleasant in the cool of early morning. The outlook over Calpe and the Penõn de Ifach is superb, with the Mediterranean stretching away into the wide blue yonder. The crag can get rather busy at times and parking can be a problem (as can turning round), a little forethought and consideration for others might save inflaming those of a Latin temperament.

Access (see Map Page 35)

Follow the directions for Toix West into the Maryvilla Complex (by the Michelin man). At the first junction turn left, (right leads up to Toix West) at the second junction fork right. The next junction is a triple one, take the central road. At the fourth junction turn left and at the fifth turn right. The road dips down into a minor valley and then rises around a bend to arrive suddenly at the cliff. Beware of traffic coming the other way on this final narrow section. It is possible to turn round a couple of hundred metres beyond the cliff at a slight widening in the road, but there is a mighty drop to the left.

The routes are described from right to left starting at a short quarried wall that rises from the tarmac. This is perhaps the ultimate roadside crag.

THE YELLOW ROUTE   VS   5a   40ft.   *Led Dec '92*
Another route with an inspiring name. Start at the right side of the wall where it is slabby. The climb follows a curious twisting groove.

Gain the groove awkwardly and follow it using advanced bridging techniques until a couple of delicate steps lead to the final bolt, (the one with a big arrow painted next to it). Either lower off this or top out and scramble down to the right.

Across the road a pair of big bolts allow abseil access to ADIOS DALI, according to the inscription on the rock the Spanish grade is 8a-, the English equivalent should be of the order of E verybignumbers 6 andabit.

VIA NUTS   E3   5c   50ft.
This is the route between the right-hand YELLOW ROUTE and GRAPHIC WHORE. As the name suggests the protection is ethically pure.

GRAPHIC WHORE   E3   6a   50ft.
Climbs the steep, blunt arête by a sustained series of moves. The name is sometimes painted on the rock but because of a local feud it may have been obliterated. If this is the case the bolt runners can be identified by the blue rings painted around them. If the bolts are missing you had better go and do something else.

Difficult delicate climbing leads to below a small roof. Layback round this to gain a big pocket, the only good hold on the climb. Either continue up to the right to the top of the cliff, or jump off and lower off the last bolt.

GOING SOLO   E3   6a   40ft.
Another route that undergoes periodic changes in its status. Start a couple of metres left of the arête of GRAPHIC WHORE, at (possibly) a line of three bolts.

A problem start to a letter box gives way to sustained face climbing on small edges and sidepulls leading to a pair of lowering bolts.

The next feature to the left is a right slanting bay in the cliff face formed by a series of shallow sandy caves filled with grotesque flowstone. This has been climbed but should have been left. A line of green painted bolts crosses this feature from right to left to give an altogether better climb.

THE GREEN ROUTE   *   HVS   5b   70ft.   *Dec '92*   *2nd*

A couple of tricky moves lead to easier climbing up into the caves (slippery rock and an optional thread). Swing left then climb steeply up the crack above, with strenuous moves where it bulges. Pull out left onto easier angled rock that leads to the top and lowering bolts.

To the left is a large cave from which a fossilised dinosaur peeks. Beyond this is a steep brown pockety wall that gives some of the best pitches on the cliff, though blinkers might be needed on some of the lower sections. The first route starts at a thin crack that rises steeply to the right and contains a couple of old nails/pegs.

EL OSO Y EL MADRONO   **   E2   5c   90ft.

A good pitch on unusual holds. It is rather easier and rather better protected than initial appearances might suggest.

    Make a couple of moves up the thin crack then step left onto the wall and climb up to a large pocket and optional thread. A little higher trend diagonally to the right until a long step to the right leads to a large, well hidden hole. Now climb straight up on flowstone "snappies" until it is possible to step left to below a hanging flake from where there are two possibilities. If you are feeling lucky and the flake is still there pull over the roof and continue direct. Otherwise step left and finish up VIA YOYOBA.

DESCENT. By abseil or walking down to the right.

KING CUCUDRULU   *   E4   6b   80ft.

This cuts out the deviation to the right on the parent route by climbing straight up the wall past two big black bolts using some holds that are "so small they ain't no holds at all." Join VIA YOYOBA and lower off the 'pig's tail' on the left.

VIA YOYOBA   ***   E2   5c   90ft.   *Led En.*

A gem of a pitch that gives steep climbing on mostly good holds. Start left of centre of the wall directly below a vertical keyhole-shaped pocket at 50ft.

Mantelshelf awkwardly onto a thin finger ledge and climb to the first bolt. Step left into a shallow scoop and make a couple of hard moves up this to easier rock. Now step right and climb steeply to the aforementioned pocket. An odd squatted rest is possible in this feature. When you are suitably recovered traverse horizontally to the right, avoiding the temptation to try and climb straight up, until a blind reach gains a huge hidden jug. Pull up then follow the much easier groove to the top. Descend by abseil.

SOL I BON TEMPS ** E3 6a 80ft.
A good pitch that makes the most of the left side of the wall. The climbing is quite sustained but has a fierce fingery crux. Start just left of the thin finger ledge that marks the start of VIA YOYOBA and below the left most of three bolts in a triangle.

Climb straight up to the bolt and pass it with difficulty to join YOYOBA at its easy section. Continue up and left to a "pigeon hole" then make difficult moves on painful pockets up and left again to easier ground. Now amble up the ramp on the right to a final couple of steep moves to a lowering station on the edge of the wall. A 165ft (50m) rope will just allow you to get back to the ground from here.

The next feature to the left is one of the major ones of the wall, a prominent diagonal line of large pockets and holes rising leftwards to a conspicuous cave. This is the line of:

VIA PYRAMIDE ** VS 150ft.
Start at the foot of the diagonal line just to the right of the step in the ground at the foot of the cliff.
1.   80ft.   4c.   Follow the line of large holes, all rather floral at first, with intermittent protection from assorted pegs and threads. The climbing involves making awkward moves between vast jugs until respite is possible at the cave stance. Bolt and thread belays.
2.   70ft.   5a.   Make a few difficult moves above the stance until it is possible to move left onto the exposed face (bolt runner on the Green Route). Continue leftwards to finish up the edge of the wall in a fine position, or the easier and inferior groove around to the left.

Originally the route finished by traversing across the rugged slab on the right of the belay. (5a)

DESCENT. Up and right of the top of the climb is an abseil anchor allowing a 120ft abseil back to base. Beware of people climbing below.

The final three routes in this area are reached by scrambling up the earth step to get to the foot of an attractive grey slab.

THE SILVER ROUTE * E1 5c 130ft. *Led Dec '92*

A route with some difficult but well protected moves on the right side of vertical.

Start below the line of silver bolts, (obvious really).

The lower section of the climb gives sustained moves on small, sharp holds until the diagonal break on PYRAMIDE is reached. After a quick blow, step right on to the steeper wall. Thankfully the increase in angle is compensated for by a corresponding increase in the size of the handholes (yes handholes), so press on up into the easier finishing corner.

DESCENT. Abseil from the belay or from better anchors up to the left. 120ft to the ground.

LA FINA ** VS 120ft.

In the centre of the grey slab is a vague scoop with occasional pink spots. Start below this. Carry a few medium to large rocks.

1.   60ft.   4c.   Climb up the centre of the scoop with sustained interest to a thread and bolt belay in the cave.

2.   60ft.   5a.   Above the stance is a corner up which the route finishes. Gain this by a difficult move using a one finger pocket (on a VS!). Once gained, the corner gives steep and steady moves to the summit. Move left to a belay and abseil anchor.

THE GREEN ROUTE * HVS 5b 110ft.

The final climb takes the left edge of the slab and the steeper wall above.

Follow the line of bolts up the steep slab. As they become more spaced the climbing gets easier despite appearances to the contrary. Continue up ever-steepening rock on ever-improving holds to reach a stance on top of the wall with bolt belays.

DESCENT is by a 120ft abseil from the belay.

The other section of rock that contains routes at Toix East is the impressively smooth piece of rock a couple of hundred metres up the hillside from the roadside crag. It is approached by walking along the road until a small path winds up through the undergrowth to arrive at a shallow cave below the wall. The routes are described from right to left again.

DESCENT from all routes is by a 120ft abseil from bolts above the centre of the wall.

The first route starts a short distance to the right of the cave.

THE GREY RIB   **   E3   6a   120ft.
Climb up to a thin in situ thread then make harder moves to a big bolt. Pass this avoiding any Conservative tendencies, to reach slightly easier climbing. The bulge above is passed on excellent small finger holders above which more reasonable moves lead to a small bay. One awkward move gives access to jugs allowing a quick pull onto easier ground. The belay lies a short distance above and left.

VIA DE LOS FAKIROS   ***   E3   6a   120ft.
An excellent fingery pitch, even more fun than lying on a bed of nails.
    Climb the crack that springs from the right side of the cave past a prominent peg, using jugs and gnarly finger jams (Rock 8 useful) until it is possible to swing left and mantel onto a pedestal. Move up to clip a bolt on the wall above (distinctly harrowing for shorties) and pass it on the right to a second bolt. Now make difficult moves left then up past two more bolts to reach the long awaited jug. Beyond this easier slabby climbing leads left to a short crack (two optional threads, not in situ) which is followed to the top.

CAVE ROUTE LEFT-HAND   ***   E3   6a   110ft.
The route starts in the cave to the left of FAKIROS. It exits left from the cave and gives sustained fingery climbing up the steepening wall and the slab above, eventually joining FAKIROS. Almost as good as its more famous namesake.

A line up the slab to the left of the cave has some pathetic attempts at chipped holds and an unfinished line of bolts that do not reach the ground. Further to the left is a vertical elongated pocket a short distance up the wall, this is gained by the next route.

FLUID CONNECTION   ***   E3   6a   120ft.
Another fine piece of climbing with a steep lower section giving way to open slab climbing above.

From the starting block sprint up the lower wall, past threads and a bolt to gain the recess above. Move delicately right at one of two levels into a shallow groove and climb this steeply on its left side (crux) to a resting place at the foot of the upper slab. This gives excellent climbing up its centre with rather spaced protection, leading to a final easy groove.

FLUID CONNECTION LEFT   **/*   E3   6a   120ft.
Rather harder and a little less satisfying than the original (and best) route.

Follow the previous route in to the recess. Now climb the small red pillar on the left to its top. The bulge above is passed by swinging right on to the wall and back left a couple of moves higher to reach a good thread. Either abseil/lower off this (*) or step right into the centre of the slab to join and follow the parent route to the top (**).

There are a couple of short routes further to the left but they are not fully equipped at the present time.

PENON DE IFACH, 1079ft (329m)

The "Penon" is the unmistakable lump of rock that sticks out of the sea between the two beaches at Calpe, towering over the harbour. It looks for all the world like a volcanic plug, and it is described as such in some travel guides, but in fact the rock is coralline limestone. The summit is a worthy objective for an afternoon's stroll, taking an easy hour from the harbour. There is a well made path throughout and the scenery is excellent with good views of the north face climbs, of the excellent beach of the Playa Levante, and of the mountains inland. The summit offers a fine panorama in all directions and has several comfortable bivi sites for those who would like to see the sun rise out of the Mediterranean. Brocken Spectres are a common phenomenon when a sea mist is blowing on to the land.

Although all sides of the Penón are rocky, the climbing is concentrated in two main areas. These are very different in character and are described separately.

The South Face

This vast wall of rock is over a thousand feet high, riddled with cave systems and has colossal overhangs crossing large sections of the cliff.

The left side of the face is flanked by a huge barrel-shaped buttress that awaits development. This runs rightwards to form a relatively easy angled slab that provides a remarkably reasonable route, the VIA VALENCANOS, up this imposing cliff. Further right a conspicuous shallow twisting groove and flake system runs almost the full height of the cliff and is taken by the classic DIEDRE U.P.S.A. Further right still the cliff becomes a complex mass of ramps, walls and overhangs through which a variety of routes weave their way, some using the odd bit of aid, (tut tut). Beyond this the cliff continues for a considerable distance rising straight from the sea.

The rock on this face is very variable though it is mostly solid on the routes described. The in situ gear is often not as good as you may have come to expect in Spain, so it is worth carrying a comprehensive rack. Any of the routes can be done comfortably in an afternoon by a competent party but bivouacs are not an uncommon experience. The message is clear - if in doubt start early. A leisurely afternoon on the beach is vastly more pleasant than an epic on the face in the gathering gloom.

Despite these rather grim warnings the south face of the Penõn brings a different aspect to the climbing hereabouts and any visitor should sample at least one of the routes at the appropriate grade. You should enjoy it and if not, at least you will have ticked the experience.

Access

Drive to the harbour in Calpe (you can't miss it, it is just below that big rock!) then continue along the road until it bends right on to the sea wall. A dirt track continues out to below the face, the first close-up views of which are impressive; many teams get no closer! Park here, although if there are any disreputable looking types around it is worth considering leaving the car at the harbour and walking the last few hundred metres.

For VIA SAME scramble straight up to the foot of the barrel-shaped buttress at the left of the face. For all the other routes go almost to the end of the dirt track to find a faint path that goes up loose earth and rock (just before the quarried section of the wall) until right under the cliff. Here it improves and ascends steeply leftwards under all the routes. At an easing in the gradient there is a conspicuous diagonal crack rising to the right, this is the start of VIAS ANGLADA-GALLEGO and GOMEZ-CANO. A little further left is a steep flow-stone wall sprouting a line of big rusty bolts; the first pitch of VIA MANUEL. Left again is the well trodden area directly below the flake of DIEDRE U.P.S.A. and finally the red bay below the great grey slab taken by VIA VALENCANOS.

The routes are described as approached on this path, that is RIGHT to LEFT.

Descent

From the top of the hill a good footpath zig-zags down the north-east face (or take the shorter rougher direct route halfway round the zig-zag) to a tunnel which pops out under the north-west face a short distance above the town. About 30 minutes is adequate to get back down. Because of the complex structure and large size of the south face, abseil descents are an all time bad idea, except in a total emergency.

The Climbs

There is a girdle of the sea cliff section of the Penón starting at the end of the dirt track, EL TRAVERSA NAUTICO. This is reputed to be about HVS but the first pitch at least looks like a full blown aid extravaganza with lots of old rusty bolts and tatty bits of rope (pendulum points?) littering the wall up to 40ft above the sea. On a hot, calm day it may repay a visit by anyone with a panache for horizontal soloing as long as they don't mind a wetting.

The first 'proper' route is:

VIA ANGALADA-GALLEGO ** E2 1030ft.
A long route that climbs the centre of the face. It passes to the left of the central cave system and finishes the notch between the twin summits of the Penón. Most of the difficult climbing is on the lower section of the route with things easing as height is gained.

Start a short distance down the slope from the foot of the conspicu-ous rightward rising crack line taken by VIA GOMEZ-CANO. The name is painted on the rock.

1. 110ft. 5b. Climb straight up the wall on Gogarth-like rock to gain the crack about 60 feet up. Follow the crack to the right with difficulty to gain an uncomfortable hanging stance with an array of belays.
2. 130ft. 5c. Continue rightward until forced to climb straight up the wall following the pegs. Eventually a traverse to the right leads into a corner, a short distance up which is a good stance.
3. 70ft. Follow the corner easily to gain the great cave system, an impressive spot.
4. 130ft. 5b. Move left in to a corner system which is rather strenuous. At its top move left into another corner which increases in difficulty as it is climbed. Belay in a recess at the top of the corner.

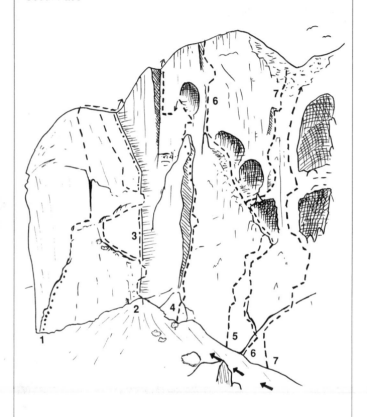

PENON DE IFACH
South Face

1. Via Same
2. Via Valencianus
3. Polvos Magicos
4. Diedro U.P.S.A.
5. Via Manuel
6. Via Gomez - Cano
7. Via Angalada - Gallego

Dave Spencer on P.8 Via Gomez - Cano (E2 5b), Penõn de Ifach

5.   80ft.   5b.   Climb the groove on the left to a pedestal stance.

6.   130ft.   5b.   Traverse right to get into a long corner system. This is taken directly and gives pleasant climbing until it rears up. A few steep moves out to the right leads to a good stance at the foot of the final easy gully line.

7.   80ft.   Plod up the groove.

8.   140ft.   More easy climbing with the odd severe move gains height quickly.

9.   160ft.   Continue to the col. The summit lies five minutes away to the left, otherwise scramble down the back to join the descent path.

VIA GOMEZ-CANO   ***   E2 & A1   1110ft.

An excellent expedition climbing the cliff at its highest point. The climbing is varied, on good rock and follows a strong natural line. The small amount of aid required on pitch 3 adds to, rather than detracts from the experience. It can be done using a couple of slings for footloops.

Start at the foot of the most obvious rightward rising crack line.

1.   130ft.   5b.   Follow the crack up to the right strenuously to an easing in the angle. Now follow the flake system that trends back to the left by undercutting, jamming and bridging. Eventually a big new bolt in the right wall is reached, either finger traverse past this (safe but a move of 5c), or climb a little higher and stride out right (easier but a little bolder). Both ways lead to a sloping stance and a selection of belays.

2.   50ft.   5a.   Climb the groove above the stance past an awkward bulge (big bolt on the right) to another sloping ledge.

3.   130ft.5b. & A1. Gain the groove awkwardly and climb it past a couple of old pegs until it is possible to trend right up the wall by sustained and occasional blind moves. Steeper climbing straight up the wall leads to the bottom of a slanting crack sprouting a row of pegs. Aid up these (all very traditional) until it is possible to pull into the base of the giant cave system. Thread and high bolt belay.

Colin Binks getting technical on Pa Roig (E2 5c), Gandia

4.   70ft.   4c.   Climb up to the right then traverse to the left towards the arête of the cave. Ascend this on fossiliferous dinosaur dongo to a stance in a bay.

5.   120ft.   4b.   Step left and climb the rib (avoiding looking down) to a major change in atmosphere. Amble up the rough grey slabs to a belay in a dusty hollow.

6. & 7.250ft.   Continue up and left on easy ground to the apex of the cave system to a belay below a corner crack.

(NOTE: at this point DIEDRE U.P.S.A. lies a short distance down to the left. A diagonal abseil allows escape in this direction though such action may create its own problems.)

8.   100ft.   5b.   Climb the corner groove to a pedestal (possible belay on the right) then make awkward moves to get into the bulging crack above. This eases with height until it is possible to swing left to gain a comfortable ledge.

9.   130ft.   5c.   Get back into the crack system and wriggle up into the chimney above. This leads to more open climbing up cracks and grooves on the left. As the rock steepens a niche is reached, exit right from this in a position of some exposure, and follow the ramp up and right to gain a superbly situated (and rather small) stance below the final obstacle.

10.   130ft.   5b.   Climb left up slabby rock to get into the large red corner which leads with the occasional tricky move to a well pegged bulge. Undercuts enable better holds to be reached then the still steep corner is followed until a crack leads out to the left above all difficulties. The top lies 100ft above up easy rock.

VIA MANUEL   *   E3   930ft.
A character-building directissima up the centre of the giant buttress between the two biggest cave systems. Some of the rock on the lower section is rather dubious and, except for on the first pitch, the fixed gear is both thinly spread and often in a laughable condition.
    Start to the left of the prominent diagonal crack of GOMEZ-CANO below a flowstone wall which sprouts an array of old bolts and pegs.

Chris Craggs on Right Route (E3 5c), Boquer Valley, Majorca

The first pitch is often done as a climb in its own right, (bottom end E3 5c ***).

1.   140ft.   5c.   Climb straight up the butch wall following the line of old aid gear. As height is gained the protection becomes a little more spaced but the climbing gradually eases, (always assuming that you don't run out of steam) until it is possible to move right to a groove. Up this past a large loose-looking 'tooth' to a restricted stance and multiple belays.

2.   60ft.   5b.   Climb straight up off the stance via an awkward crack until it is possible to swing right into a groove containing a line of bolts. These provide a direct aid variation that should be avoided in case you get struck down by a thunderbolt from on high. Swing right again to reach the stance above pitch two of GOMEZ-CANO.

3.   140ft.   5b.   Go up the rib above the belay or straight up the easier groove to its right. Both ways lead to the tip of a rather fragile flake from which committing and scarey moves can be made up and left to a ledge. Optional stance with poor belays. Continue up and right heading for the obvious corner crack which is followed steeply to reach the start of the cave system at the bolt and thread belays of GOMEZ-CANO.

4.   150ft.   4c.   Follow pitch 4 of GOMEZ-CANO then continue up pitch 5 to the major change in angle. Move right into a chimney, through an arch and round a rib to thread belays in a groove.

5.   130ft.   5b.   Either climb the rib right of the groove up to the bulges which are crossed leftward in spectacular fashion, or climb the rib to the left of the groove. Both ways lead to an area of slabs from which trend up and left to reach an unexpected haven, a spot to hide for a while.

6.   120ft.   5b.   Plod up the easy chimney to its closure then make difficult undercutting moves out to the right. Possible stance. Above the point of arrival is a crack sprouting a couple of old pegs (tent pegs that is). Up this then leftwards to a thread belay below a corner blocked by a big roof.

7.   90ft.   4c.   There is rumoured to be a direct finish up the impressive corner, but for those who are long overdue for a cold beer the crack on the right leads to the arête, above which another crack leads to easier ground.

8.   100ft.   4a.   Wend your way up the rough rock between the sweet smelling herbs to the top.

DIEDRO U.P.S.A.   ***   HVS   *John E   30Dec 92*

A classic climb of its type taking the continuous flake/groove line up the left side of the face. The climbing is varied and not overly exposed except for one pitch. The stances are good throughout.

Start below the impressive groove at an apron of easier angled and rather scrappy rock by a large cactus bush.

1.   50ft.   Any one of a variety of lines, easiest on the left, lead to a stance below the groove proper.

2.   100ft.   5a.   Step right into the groove and follow it steeply but on good holds past a poor stance to a better one where the groove becomes a chimney.

3.   100ft.   5b.   The right wall of the chimney is climbed steeply on a rather odd mixture of 'stuck on' holds. This is the crux of the route and is best done quickly. As soon as it is possible to bridge across to the opposite wall things become easier. Continue to another well sheltered stance.

4.   80ft.   5a.   Keep on trucking up the corner stystem until it becomes blocked.

5.   100ft.   4b.   Move right to gain the slab, then traverse back left to gain the line which has now become a mighty ravine. Amble up this to a shady belay behind a pinnacle. It is possible to traverse left from here to gain the final corner, but this is hardly cricket and it eliminates the best part of the route.

6.   80ft. 4c/5b.   or somewhere in between depending on stature. Climb to a block jammed behind the top of the pinnacle then make a difficult move (or an easy move) up the wall above. Fine climbing now leads up and right across the wall to gain a chimney which is reached all too soon. Up this to a belay.

7.   80ft.   Continue up into the huge cave from which all exits look closed. Scramble left to a massive bunch of tat.

8.   70ft.   After arguing about who is going to go first, abseil or get lowered (how good is your mate's belaying anyway?) down the wall to reach the end of a ledge, you will have to open your eyes for this last bit. The far end of the ledge contains several stout

anchors, from which point you can discuss methods of getting the second across.

9. 100ft. 4b. Move left and climb the groove to a shrubby stance, below a steeper section of a corner.

10. 120ft. 4c. The rather impressive final obstacle can be bypassed by a bit of wide bridging, the climbing then eases rapidly to arrive at a notch in the ridge, twin bolt belay.

From here the summit ridge lies a short distance above and is reached by the easy angled corner on the left.

VIA VALENCIANOS *** Hard Severe 820ft.

A classic climb taking the easiest line up an impressive face. Technical difficulties are not excessive except for a couple of well-protected moves on pitch three. In the event of unforeseen difficulties abseil retreat is straightforward as the stances lie in a straight line even though the climbing wanders a bit. Carry a few medium to large rocks to supplement the in situ protection.

Start in a red bay below the right corner of the great grey buttress that abuts the left side of the main face. The name is painted on the left wall of the bay.

1. 110ft. 3a. Climb up and right then back left (all a bit loose) before going straight up to reach a smooth slab with a peg in it. Step awkwardly right and continue up easier rock to a good ledge and three bolt belay below a big smooth corner (don't worry: it doesn't go up there).

2. 120ft. Traverse to the left, passing an optional stance then climb up to gain a slanting herbaceous border. Graze your way up this then climb the short arête and a blocky crack above to reach a ledge which is followed back to the right to a stance directly above the previous one.

3. 100ft. 4b. Climb easily up the corner until it steepens. The slabby crack in the right wall of the main corner above is the crux, it gives a couple of difficult bridging moves well protected by an in situ Friend and thread. Once a jug on the right wall is grasped things ease. Continue up the corner until it is possible to traverse left to a stance below the great slab.

4. 70ft. 4a. A tricky start leads to easier climbing trending

Sherri Davy well chuffed at the top of Via Valencianos (H.S.)
Penõn de Ifach

left to a small stance and single bolt belay with bush for a back up.

5.   150ft.   3c.   Cruise up the slab. There is an option stance by a bush at 70ft (nut belays). Otherwise run it out to a stance sat astride the ridge. Superb views in all directions.

6.   100ft.   4b.   Walk (or crawl) along the ridge back to the mountain then traverse left along a ledge until just short of a bush. Climb the flaky crack in the grey slab (peg) and pass the bulge on good holds. Slightly easier but rather inferior variations exist to the left. Belay a little higher on a nail!

7.   70ft.   Up rightwards keeping to the clean rock to a 2 bolt belay in a notch (the top of U.P.S.A. - impressive views downwards).

8.   100ft.   Amble up the groove on the left to arrive, well chuffed, on the summit ridge.

POLVOS MAGICOS   **   HVS   680ft.
This route, which is low in the grade, follows the big corner system right of the slab of VALENCIANOS, with which it shares several stances. A good direct line with optional escape routes leftwards. Take a light rack.

1.   100ft.   As for VALENCIANOS pitch 1.

2.   80ft.   5a.   Straight up the smooth corner, with bolts, pegs and as many nuts as you want, a fine sustained pitch.

3.   100ft.   4b.   As for VALENCIANOS pitch 3.

4.   70ft.   4c.   Start as for VALENCIANOS pitch 4 but continue straight up into the corner system. Follow this to a belay in a niche.

5.   90ft.   5a.   Straight on up the corner via varied climbing and the odd bit of dubious rock to a bolt belay on the ridge.

6.   60ft.   4c.   Up the groove above the end of the ridge to reach bulges that are passed on the left in an exposed position, this leading to easy ground.

7./8. 170ft.   Finish easily as for VALENCIANOS.

The final route on the south side of the Penōn takes the prominent chimney crack in the right side of the barrel-shaped buttress to the left of the main face.

VIA SAME   *   E3   780ft.

An interesting but devious route that is unfortunately rather unbalanced, with a difficult lower section and much easier climbing above. Start well to the left of the upper crack system at a cave with a crack rising from its left side.

1.   50ft.   5c.   Gain the crack steeply and follow it strenuously to a stance at the foot of a corner/ramp.

2.   80ft.   6a.   Climb the corner with considerable difficulty (pegs) and belay where the angle becomes much more amenable.

3.   60ft.   4a.   Follow the ramp to the right easily (at least in comparison to what has gone before) to a large stance and belay at the foot of a crack leading to an imposing chimney line. Those who have a fear of enclosed spaces can and should escape to the right from here onto VIA VALENCIANOS.

4.   80ft.   5b.   Climb the steep awkward crack until it opens out in to a chimney, graunch your way up this to a stance in the bowels of the earth.

5.   140ft.   5a.   Continue thrashing upwards until the chimney narrows and more open climbing (now with the tattered remains of an expensive suntan) leads to a belay on easier angled rock.

6.   100ft.   4b.   Up the pleasant slabs to a belay on the ridge in common with VIA VALENCIANOS.

From here either finish up VALENCIANOS pitches 6, 7, and 8 (270ft) or abseil down the lower part of the same route in 3 or 4 rope lengths, always giving due consideration to those having the epic of their lives on the way up.

North-West Face

Character

This is the large dome-shaped white face that directly overlooks the harbour. There is a variety of routes here that are in the shade for most of the day. From Easter onwards the face gets the sun in the evenings, so later in the year an option exists depending on weather conditions. The rock is strangely smooth and covered with a white dusty lichen; two factors which combine to make the climbing an altogether more delicate exercise than is found on the other crags in this guide; a nice contrast that should be sampled.

The routes can be divided into two types; longer affairs on the higher right side of the face requiring a selection of nuts and shorter bolt protected routes centred around the fine white wall 50m right of the tunnel entrance.

Approaches

Follow the normal walking route for the Penõn from the harbour, starting at some broad steps opposite the BAR GAVIOTA. This takes about 20 minutes. It is also possible to park further up the hill at an isolated small car park by an odd small square tower, cutting about 5 minutes off the walk, but ensure that you will be back to the car by dusk. The path zig-zags gently up the hillside, though more direct versions are possible for the fit, and passes below all of the route on the final 'zag' up to the tunnel entrance.

Descent

For the routes on the right side of the face scramble the short distance to the summit and descend by the regular path. For the climbs on the left side either abseil back down the line of the climb or top out on to the ridge and scramble down the back to reach the uphill end of the tunnel, 10 minutes back to the base of the climbs.

The climbs are described as approached on the footpath on the way up the hill, that is from RIGHT to LEFT. The first route starts a short distance above the path at the left side of the big buttress dropping

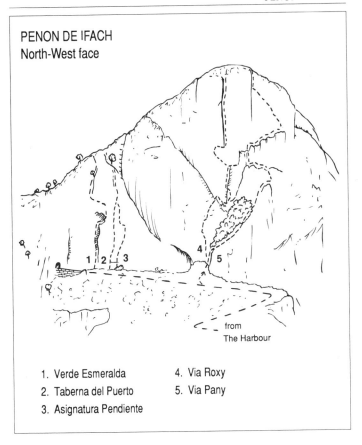

PENON DE IFACH
North-West face

from
The Harbour

1. Verde Esmeralda
2. Taberna del Puerto
3. Asignatura Pendiente
4. Via Roxy
5. Via Pany

from the summit, at a narrow chimney. This is reached by a thin track branching right off the main path.

VIA PANY ** Severe 710ft.
An interesting climb at a very reasonable standard up an imposing part of the Penón. Not of the calibre of VALENCIANOS but well worthwhile, (and it is usually in the shade). The climbing is rather

73

vegetated in the lower part but improves as height is gained to give a grand upper section. Carry a light rack and a few slings.

1.   80ft.   3c.   Climb the steep awkward chimney on polished pockets passing a thread on the right wall to a belay on a good ledge above on the right.

2.   150ft.   Easy scrambling leads up right following a well marked trail through the shrubbery to a belay on top of the first buttress.

3.   110ft.   3b.   Follow the prominent rib to its top then traverse left easily to a stance below a corner.

4.   70ft.   3b.   Up the interesting corner moving left to a belay amongst blocks.

5.   100ft.   More easy climbing with the odd awkward step leads up and right along the ledge system running across the face to a stance at the highest point of the second buttress.

6.   100ft.   3a.   Above the stance a slab leads left to reach a large crack falling from the summit. Follow this in a fine position to a stance and belay 40ft up the crack system.

7.   100ft.   3c.   Follow the crack throughout. It is awkward low down but the angle and the difficulties ease as height is gained. Belay on easy ground, the summit lies a little higher.

Note there are easier variations to the top section available further to the right.

VIA ROXY   **   E3   780ft.
A rather indifferent lower section leads to impressive climbing up the great crack system that falls from the left side of the summit dome. The crux is hard but very well protected and eminently frigable. Carry a standard rack, with a few extra large hexes or Friends.
Start as for the previous route.

1.   100ft.   5a.   From the chimney at the foot of PANY slant left up rock and two veg. to reach the prominent jamming crack. Bridge this! to a ledge (bolt) and make a couple of awkward moves around to the left to a stance and nut belays below a wider crack.

2.   60ft.   5a.   Bridge elegantly up the corner past threads (or get an arm and leg in and give it some grunting), to a stance on a good

ledge a little higher, nut belays.

3.   110ft.   5a.   Climb the wall above the stance for 25ft then slant up to the right over flakes and blocks to reach the huge ramp that crosses the face, at a pair of bolts. Descend for 25ft to a good stance at two old bolts.

4.   100ft.   5a.   Climb over (or up) the palm tree on the right then move right to a corner. Climb this past big pegs to a steeper corner which is bridged past the world's biggest wooden wedge, (how the hell did they get that up there; the mind boggles). A short distance above is a ledge and bolt belay, with peg back ups around the corner. Escape is possible here up to the right to join PANY at the end of pitch 4.

5.   90ft.   6a.   Follow the line of threads across the left wall (great photos) and up to a ledge. Move back right and make a difficult but well protected mantelshelf to reach the break, shuffle right and make more difficult moves to gain the crack above. This leads more easily to a restricted stance.

6.   80ft.   5b.   Up the steep crack above, a bit of a thrash to start with and then excellent bridging and jamming leads to a stance on a pedestal on the left.

7.   80ft.   5a.   Continue up the groove and crack line to arrive at a twin bolt belay, the best fixed gear on the route.

The top lies 170ft above and is most easily reached on the right.

To the left are a vast series of steep walls and soaring grooves containing the odd relic of aid attempts.

The next routes lie 100m further up the main track where a fine, clean white wall descends within a couple of metres of the path. There are three fine climbs here with some scope for mixing and matching.

The right side of the face has a shrubby groove running up into steeper rock, from this a left slanting crack, containing a prominent thread, heads towards the centre of the face.

Start under this groove.

VAMPIRO   **   E5   250ft.

A taxing series of pitches especially if the easier variations are shunned.

1.   80ft.   6a.   Climb the groove then move left to gain the slanting crack. This is followed until it is possible to head straight up the wall on good but spaced holds and pockets (continuing up the crack to join the next route is a cop out). A few rather more difficult moves lead to easier rock trending left to the stance in the centre of the face shared with ASIGNATURA PENDIENTE.

2.   90ft.   6a/6b.   Climb up to the right to gain the right-hand bolt line running up the crest of a blunt rib. Follow this with sustained difficulty until it becomes 'blank.' It is apparently possible to continue straight up following the bolts (6b or more), it is certainly possible to head left to gain the parallel line of bolts. Both ways lead to a small stance and a five bolt belay!

3.   80ft.   6a.   Step right and follow yet another line of bolts with (you guessed it) difficulty to eventually gain a slab and very substantial tree belay.

DESCENT. Either abseil back down the face in two rope lengths, 80ft first then 160ft, or scramble left to get over the ridge then walk down the back to the tunnel.

ASIGNATURA PENDIENTE   ***   E3   250ft.

A great route following the centre of the wall giving three contrasting pitches.

Start behind a bush just above the path, below the right end of an overlap 12ft up.

1.   80ft.   5c.   Gain and cross the overlap then climb up to the left to reach a crack that slants to the right crossing a series of bulges. This gives strenuous climbing until an awkward pull gains the easy groove leading to a good stance and multiple belays.

2.   90ft.   6a.   Move right to reach the leftmost of a pair of bolt lines. These are followed over a bulge and up a shallow groove until it steepens and blanks out. Difficult moves and perhaps a small dyno now lead up and left to better holds (hidden from below) then up and left again to a long flake crack that leads to a small stance and five bolt

belay. (The Spaniards do not do things by halves.)

3.   80ft.   5b.   Climb up above the stance until forced left into the chimney. This has an awkward exit and leads to easier crack climbing with the odd tricky move to reach a big tree belay.

DESCENT as for the previous route.

TABERNA DEL PUERTO   ***   E5   170ft.

A difficult and sustained second pitch is the highlight of this route although the initial slab is not without interest.

Start just off the footpath at the left side of the slab where a steep wall bars access to a line of bolts.

1.   70ft.   6a.   A problem start gains the slab, a couple of easier moves then some difficult smearing leads to the overlap, which is crossed rightwards. Better holds lead to a barrier of steeper rock which is passed on good holds to a small stance with a selection of belays.

2.   100ft.   6a.   Move up the ramp on the right then follow the bolts straight up the wall, this section gives superb sustained climbing with the odd 'gripper clip.' Difficult moves into a shallow niche provide the crux and are followed by some seemingly reckless laybacking up a flake system to better holds (not before time). Move right to the five bolt stance.

Three options now present themselves:

1,   for gluttons, move right and do battle with the top pitch of VAMPIRO (6a).

2,   for those looking for a pleasant contrast, plod up the top pitch of ASIGNATURA PENDIENTE (5b).

3,   for those who feel they have done more than enough, the ground is 160ft away and the beach is 10 minutes beyond. Go for it!

The final route ascends the great groove system that bounds the smooth white face on the left. It is further recognised by having a short flight of stone steps leading to a tiny cave (which doubles as the local rubbish dump) at its foot.

VERDE ESMERALDA ** E1 280ft.

An interesting trip through some weird and wonderful rock scenery.

1. 90ft. 4c. Climb the steps (technically very reasonable) then fight through the bushes to gain the groove. A variety of routes lead up, over and through the rock to a comfortable grotto, a real des. res.

2. 70ft. 5c. Move to the right edge of the cave and grapple with the bulges above, 'big odds' and 'big freds' lead rapidly to easier ground (or even more rapidly back into the cave). Move left below the bulges to a good stance.

3. 120ft. 5a. The crack and corner system above is followed throughout with the odd moment of interest to gain the ridge.

DESCENT. The back entrance to the tunnel lies five minutes down to the left.

Round to the left of and below the lower end of the tunnel is a huge leaning crag of superb looking white rock. Anybody bored by the Central Wall at Malham and not too keen on the sun could spend a happy month or two beavering away down there.

PENYA ROTJA DE MARXUQUERA

Note: Henceforth, for reasons that should be obvious, I will refer to this crag as 'GANDIA.'

Character
A superbly situated cliff in a quiet valley a few kilometres to the west of the large town of Gandia. The routes are generally short, up to 80ft and are very well protected by bolts and in situ threads. There are almost invariably lowering stations consisting of large bolts with steel rings installed where the angle relents. There is a variety of styles of climbing varying from the brutish overhangs of the Sector Hydraulics, to the open more delicate fare of the Sector Critic on the left-hand crag.

The crag faces due south and is in the sun all day but with shelter provided by the larger roofs for those who have already seen too much of it. The outward view over the orange orchards is superb, it is little wonder the locals call the place 'paradise.'

Approaches
If these directions are followed closely the crag is easy to find; any attempts at short cuts may well end up with you being lost forever in bandit country.

From Calpe follow the N332 northwards to Benisa. It is possible to continue along the N332 all the way to Gandia but this is very slow due to the narrow roads and the heavy goods traffic. Therefore just to the north of Benisa get on to the N7 motorway and follow it north, towards Valencia. After 30 km leave the motorway following the signs for Oliva, Alquera and Gandia. At the N332 turn left and follow the road into Gandia (about 8 km). After crossing the river pick up signs for Albaida. Follow these, (all a bit 'round the houses') until you come to a major road crossing your path. This is the Passies des Germains and is unmistakable as it is a dual carriageway with a pedestrian precinct and lines of trees running down the centre. Turn right and continue straight down this road passing a couple of roundabouts until the road bends right and appears to dwindle into a minor track. Follow this small road under the motorway and up into the valley. After only a couple of kilometres there is a minor right turn signed Raco de Tomba Marxuquera Alta. This is taken until it is possible to park just beyond a dried up river bed. The path up to the crag is reached through the orange bushes (they are green actually) and is a short, steep scramble, equivalent to about one-third of a Cromlech. The path arrives at the main (right-hand) crag, the left-hand crag is at the same level along a terrace two minutes to the left.

The climbs are described on the Main Crag first from LEFT to RIGHT. The first area is known as the "Sector Hydraulics" for obvious reasons.

PEQUENO SALTAMONTES   E3   6b   50ft.

Start at the left rim of the arches and make steep fingery moves up and right past three closely spaced bolts, as soon as the angle eases romp up to the solitary but substantial belay bolt.

To the right a peculiar tube runs up through the cliff, it may be of interest to budding gynaecologists, climbers who suffer from agoraphobia or cavers who are having withdrawal symptoms. Right again is a line of bolts leading to a cave over the lip of the overhang.

ASESINO DE VAMPIROS   **   E5   6b   60ft.

Follow the line of bolts and threads up the wall and over the bulges to the sanctuary of the cave. Either lower off or move left to the belay on the previous route and do the same.

Right again the overhangs become even bigger and contain two small caves. The next route gains the left one.

QUIEN MALONDA, MAL ACABA   ***   E5   6a   60ft.

An excellent trip into upside down land. Gain the cave from below, an ungainly rest is possible half in and half out of it. When ready head out left on good holds onto the head wall, unfortunately as the angle decreases so does the size of the holds. A fierce pull on a finger jam

Sector de Dalt

Sector Critic

Access Routes

Sector Hydraulics

Sector Vici

Sector Borrachera

PENYA ROTJA DE MARXUQUERA - GANDIA

should bring better holds in reach, followed rapidly by the belay. If not, return to the start and ponder the prospect of a slip off the first holds with the rope where it is now!

Just to the right is a line of small (artificial ?) finger holds leading leftwards up the wall, these are the start of KORTATU, maybe E6/7 6c.

BLANIULUS GUTTULATUS ** E4 6b 60ft.
Gain the right-hand cave from the left, this is a much more comfy spot than its near neighbour. When you are bored with its interior make difficult moves to reach the jugs that lurk just around the lip. Easier

moves on 'biffos' lead to the belay.

Just to the right is OSTIA COQUETA which may have been free climbed, the chalk goes a long way up it but no details are known. The next feature to the right is a slabby groove that forms the right edge of the leaning wall. Starting up this is:

ZUCARICIDA *** E4 5c 70ft.
Up the ramp for a couple of moves then swing left on to the bulging wall. The pockets are followed using good but spaced holds until they end. A long reach right off an undercut brings better holds and easier angled rock. Continue to the belay by the bush above, then either lower off or better, continue up the wall (5c) to a higher lowering point.

To the right the wall steps forward and is a much more reasonable angle (only vertical). It contains a fine selection of pitches. This is the "Sector Vici," the first route starting at the left side of the wall below some pocketed bulges and just left of a line dropping from the conspicuous belay tree.

NINA DE PORCELANA ** E1 5b 45ft, 65ft or 85ft. *L 1st Jan '93*
Make steep moves to the first bolt then continue on an odd mixture of holds with both delicate and strenuous manoeuvres to reach the tree and a lowering ring. It is possible to prolong the experience by traversing left around a flake to the belay on the previous route (5a) and for those who still can't tear themselves away to continue up the wall above this to yet another belay (5c).

GORA E.T.A. ** E4 6a 45ft.
Difficult climbing though rather 'eliminatish' in nature. Start a short distance to the left of the thin crack that is the substance of PA ROIG.
    Good but well spaced holds lead over the initial bulge to gain the rib, which gives fierce moves on small pockets and thin edges to a difficult exit onto easier angled rock. All tendencies to veer left or right must be kept well in check. Either lower off the tree or move to

Chris Craggs on Nina de
                                    Porcelana (E1 5b), Gandia

the right and have a crack at the top pitch of ASQUEROSA CO-INCINDENCIA (E4 6a).

PA ROIG *** E2 5c 45ft. ⌐ Jan 93

The thin crack containing some weathered threads is followed throughout with the crux moves at one-third height where the crack closes and some small pockets are used for progress.

ASQUEROSA COINCINDENCIA ** E2 5c/E4 6a 45ft or 80ft.

The wall to the right of the thin crack of PA ROIG contains many pockets and two prominent threads.

Steep moves on big jugs gain the threads, then more difficult moves past bolts lead to an easing in the angle and a hanging belay or lowering point. An excellent second pitch, or an extension to the first one, lies up the wall above the belays. Climb to the right of the first bolt then make hard moves into and up the centre of the wall. A small roof is passed on better holds and just above are two beefy belay bolts. Lower off.

The next feature to the right is one of the major ones of the wall a broad red streak dropping from a roof 70ft up. This is the line of:

EL SOL *** E3 6a 85ft.

A great pitch sustained and interesting. Start at the left edge of a small cave.

A few steep moves gain the first bolt; if you are going to fall off clip it first! With this done, follow the line up the streak to eventually reach a poor rest below the roof. A big undercut pinch grip on the lip allows a bolt above to the clipped and finger jugs (a contradiction in terms if ever there was one) to be gained for a quick pull over. The belays are just above.

ESCORREGUDA PRECOC E4 6c 30ft.

Start in the cave and cross the roof on good holds, then levitate up the wall above the lip to reach the lowering point. All a bit much really unless you have brought your step ladders with you.

Colin Binks on Pa Roig (E2 5c), Gandia

PEYOTE DE BOTE ** E3 5c 80ft.

Up the right edge of the cave is a shallow groove containing an odd collection of old and new bolts. Climb the groove delicately until a large hole is reached. Better holds lead up the wall above to the prominent horizontal roof which is crossed centrally with difficulty, there are holds above - honestly. A short distance above is a thick but rather weathered thread; either abseil gingerly off this or attack the jungle above to reach a chiselled thread anchor (take your own sling). Either abseil off this or continue to the terrace above and descend to the left.

To the right is a leaning red wall and below it a small bay 15ft up the crag containing a tree. The red wall is taken by:

VALENTET DE VALENCIA *** E1 5b 60ft. *2nd Jan '93*

An excellent pitch that is easier than first appearances might otherwise suggest. Gain the tree in the recess and then head up the rather imposing wall. The pockets are generally excellent and more than make up for the angle, though a little forward planning is required to ensure that you do not end up 'wrong handed.' As the climbing eases move to the right to gain a recess that contains a variety of belays to lower off from.

PLACA DE ULACA ** E4 6a 60ft.

This fingery pitch climbs the grey wall to the right of the previous route. Climb up to the right of the tree to gain the steep wall. This is well bolted but the holds are small and the difficulties sustained. Press on until forced leftwards to thankfully reach the belays of the previous route.

The next three routes lie 60 metres to the right where an hour-glass-shaped pillar breaks through an otherwise overhanging wall. This is the Sector Borrachera.

The first route climbs the leaning wall 10 metres left of the pillar.

BORRACH *** E4 5c 50ft.

A good steep pitch and doubtless a 'piece of pudding' to the stronger members of the climbing fraternity though more normal mortals will find it distinctly uphill.

Gain the first bolt from the left, then move slightly right before trending left again across the bulges on good holds often hidden deep inside pockets, to reach the lowering bolts.

The next climb takes the left side of the hour-glass-shaped pillar and the bulges above.

S'AMBOSSA   *   E2   5c   40ft.
Gain the first bolt and pass it with difficulty to reach the second bolt. Above this the climbing and the angle ease rapidly.

To the right of the pillar is a bulging wall this is taken by:

DIA DE BORRACHERA   *   E2/E4   5c/6a   25ft/40ft.
The bulges contain a variety of holds, many of them not quite as good as one would like. Using these coupled with the odd heel hook cross the roof to a thread with a steel ring on it. Either lower off or if you still feel fresh attack the rather more challenging bulges above; a rapid approach may pay dividends.

The crag continues to the right for a considerable distance (Sectors Paco and Final), and contains some impressive leaning walls and a variety of unusual rock formations. At the time of writing this whole section is largely undeveloped, containing only the odd old aid route and some easy free climbs at the extreme ends of the wall. The scope for new routing, mostly at a higher grade is considerable.

To the left of the routes so far described is an easy gully that allows access to the upper tier of the cliff (Sector de Dalt), again this is relatively undeveloped with only the major lines having been done, mostly in the VS to HVS range and with rather a dearth of fixed gear. I have left these undescribed so that those bored with 'climbing by numbers' could spend a happy afternoon exploring this area.

The final area described is the Sector Critic. This is the area of rock that lies 150 metres to the left of the Sector Hydraulics and is reached by crossing the gully to the left of the main crag and following a faint path along a narrow terrace. The main feature of this part of the cliff is a big red corner (GRAN DIEDRE) and to its right a fine grey slab of perfect rock. To left and right the rock dwindles in height and contains nothing worth travelling 1500 miles for.

For convenience and ease the routes are described from LEFT to RIGHT, that is the opposite direction to the approach.

The short left arête of the wall is:
ESPOLON AMARILLO   E2   6b   20ft.
Short, sharp and safe with no route finding problems.

The left wall of the big red corner has three lines of bolts running up it, the central one being free.

VOLDRIA MORIRME   **   E4   6b   50ft.
Start right of the tree and climb up past bolts and a thread to a ledge with a smaller tree. Make a couple of moves up to the left then head up the wall to the right of the thin crack. A lowering point is available for those fortunate enough to reach it.

GRAN DIEDRE   ***   E1   5b   60ft.
The ledge at the base of the steep section of big corner is approached from the left or the right. The upper section is probably best lay-backed, though those with big fists and a high pain resistance can jam it. Move left at the top to lowering bolts.

To the right of the corner is a steep arête that forms the substance of two routes. Holds on the arête itself are shared by the routes so tandem ascents could prove interesting.

SELECTIVA   **   E4   6a   60ft.
Start under the arête at an elongated pocket which is climbed, followed by the bulges above. Continue, passing a substantial thread, into a shallow corner until it is possible to exit round to the right to a lowering point.

ESPOLON WAY ** E4 6a 60ft.

From below the right side of the arête climb the leaning wall on spaced spiky pockets until the angle eases (if this section is too taxing it is somewhat easier to climb right then step back left). Continue up the face by the arête passing a good thread and an archaic peg to more difficult moves until things ease just below the belay bolts.

MEGALOCERAS ** E5 6b 60ft.

A route with perfect protection but a desperate crux sequence. Start as for the previous route and step right to a flake or approach it much more easily from the right. Interesting moves lead up the centre of the face until things turn nasty. A thin undercut allows access to the crux, a pull on some miserably sloping pockets to reach jugs. Better holds are followed up a short wall until the belays on the left can be reached. Using the bolts to hang on and pull on makes the route into a very pleasant A1, (or is that a red point ascent?).

The centre of the grey face has a fine flake crack running up it. This is:

AGUILES *** HVS 5a 60ft. ⌐

A fine route that is something of an anomaly as it contains no fixed gear. Several medium sized Rocks are required. Gain the base of the flake easily and follow it steeply on jugs and finger jams. Protection is perfect, unless you don't put any in. At the top of the flake move up to a belay on a higher ledge. A good route for getting back into the swing of climbing back home, a grim thought.

PICCOLISSIMA *** E2 5c 60ft. ⌐

The centre of the face between the two flakes contains a prominent bolt. This is gained from directly below and passed via tricky moves (unless you are very tall), better holds lead to another bolt and the belay of the previous route.

The right side of the face has a rising flake running across it that contains two old threads.

TERRA LLIURE   **   HVS   5a   60ft.

The base of the flake is reached over easy rock and is followed pleasantly. All but the heroic might want to supplement the threads with the odd nut runner (or should that read "all but the nuts might want to supplement the threads with the odd heroic runner"). Belays are to be found to left and right of the finishing moves.

P.S.A.N.   *   E2   6a   50ft.

Midway between the previous routes and a large fallen flake is a smooth wall at 30ft sprouting a prominent bolt. Gain this from below and improvise past it to reach another bolt then ledges and a belay.

Further to the right are some short routes though none are worthy of a full description.

MAJORCA

Introduction

Although situated 200 km (125 miles) off the Spanish mainland, Majorca, the largest of the Ballearic islands, can be considered along with the Costa Blanca as a unified climbing area. Geologically the two areas are linked by the submarine ridge that extends from the Cabo de Nao at the northern extremity of the Costa Blanca, so the raw material of the sport is the same in both places. Climatically both areas are blessed with mild winters, low rainfall and bags of sunshine. Because of this the mass holiday industry has developed which now offers the discerning climber cheap travel and accommodation at just the right time of year.

Majorca (or Mallorca as the natives prefer to call it) is about the same size as Cornwall and has a resident population of 450,000, of whom over 250,000 live in Palma. The locals speak a dialect which is quite similar to the Valencian used on the Costa Blanca and is considerably different to Castilian Spanish which is the official language of Spain. The fact that all the road signs on the island are written in Castilian has obviously upset some of the locals because without exception the spellings have been changed using spray paint.

Along the northern edge of the island runs the Sierra de Tramuntana, a complex range of rocky mountains rising to 4470ft (1450m) at the Puig Major. These hills are well worth exploring and give some rough walking in wild country. June Parker's excellent little guide *Walking in Mallorca* (Cicerone Press) describes 30 tours in detail, from the gentlest of strolls through to some arduous days out.

When To Go, How To Get There and Where To Stay

As on the Costa Blanca the summer season is best avoided except by sun worshippers who do not mind getting fried in oil. In the winter months there is rather more rainfall here than on the mainland with December being the wettest month, though temperatures are agreeably warm and the rain usually comes in short, heavy showers rather

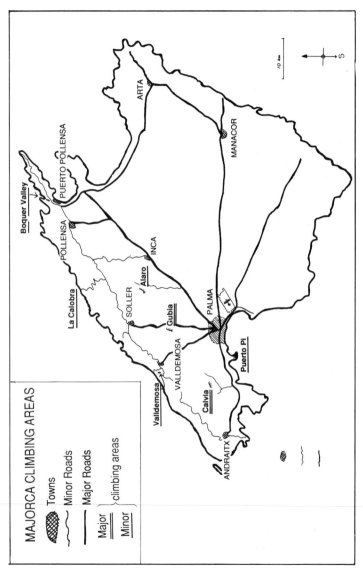

MAJORCA CLIMBING AREAS

- Towns
- Minor Roads
- Major Roads

climbing areas

Major
Minor

10 km

Boquer Valley

PUERTO POLLENSA

POLLENSA

La Calobra

SOLLER

Gubia

Alaro

INCA

ARTA

MANACOR

PALMA

Puerto Pi

VALLDEMOSA

Valldemosa

Calvia

ANDRAITX

than day-long deluges. Fortunately most of the rock dries very quickly. Any time between October and April should provide a good week's sport and a chance to beef up the remnants of your tan.

Cheap charter flights are available from all the regional U.K. airports direct to Palma throughout the winter. As pointed out in the Costa Blanca section, the prices for flights outside the school holidays are exceptionally reasonable, as are longer stays. A car is very useful on the island as a considerable amount of driving can be required especially if you intend to explore the mountains. These are best booked from the U.K. before you leave and can be picked up on arrival at the airport. It is possible to hire cars at the airport but this can be expensive. If you arrive without transport already arranged it might make economic sense to catch the airport bus into Palma and arrange something there.

Where you stay depends somewhat on the kind of holiday you have in mind. For a pure rock climbing break it is probably best to base yourself in one of the modern resorts (the Costa del Concrete) around Palma. These places are populated by the 'vino collapso' brigade in the summer but are very quiet in the winter. The beaches are superb and self-catering apartments are cheap and usually of a high standard. For those who require a total holiday, hotel accommodation with full board is available from about £7 a night in the winter. If you intend to do some walking and scrambling and would prefer to see some of old Majorca, the towns of Soller and the beautiful Puerto Pollensa are worth considering and have plenty of cheap accommodation. Consult your travel agent.

A Bit About The Climbing

As on the mainland the climbing areas are divided into two categories: older routes on the impressive mountain crags, often long and remote with little in the way of fixed gear, and newly developed smaller routes, well protected by bolts, on low-level easily accessible cliffs. The majority of the routes described here are in the latter category. All that is required are ten or so quick-draws and doubled 50 metre ropes. Only two crags have been extensively developed by British standards but even these have plenty of gaps. The other areas described are worth a short visit and have plenty of scope for new routing. For those who prefer their action to be a little more sporting there is plenty to go at up in them thar hills, or on some mighty sea cliffs.

The amount of rock that awaits development in some areas is quite staggering, there is little doubt that Majorca will become a major European centre for sport climbing in the years ahead, so if you want to make a name for yourself now is the time!

Calvia

Character

Calvia is a small crag of perfect grey limestone hidden away in a secluded valley in the wooded hills behind PALMA. The routes are generally not too steep and are very well protected by large, closely spaced bolts. The upward view of some of the climbs is rather daunting because of the compact nature of the rock, but on closer acquaintance there appears an abundance of small, sharp holds making for elegant climbing. The valley is sheltered from the elements and is a sun trap. Climbing here is all about enjoyment. In the winter the temperature can be very pleasant, though at other times of the year it can get rather too hot for comfort. Under these conditions visits will have to be very late or very early in the day with perhaps a midday break for a dip and a bit of bronzing. Many of the routes have their names painted on the rock at the crag in neat black lettering. All the climbs have substantial anchors at the top and can be done up and back to the ground on a 50m rope. Please leave any in situ gear in situ!

Access

From PALMA follow the motorway eastwards towards ANDRAITX for 13 km to a junction signed PALMA NOVA and CALVIA. The road winds up into the hills to reach the old village of CALVIA in 6 km. In the centre of the village take a right turn to the oddly named town of ESTABLISHMENTS. This narrow road is followed for $2^1/_2$ km until the stone walls at the side of the road end at a right-hand bend. It is possible to park a short distance further on. Return to the

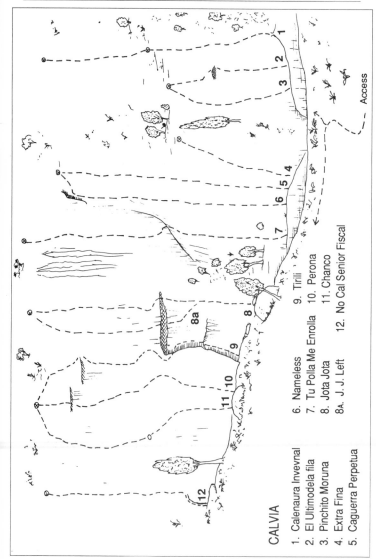

Access

Tirili
Perona
Chanco
No Cal Senior Fiscal

CALVIA

1. Calenaura Invevnal
2. El Ultimodela fila
3. Pinchito Moruna
4. Extra Fina
5. Caguerra Perpetua

6. Nameless
7. Tu Polla Me Enrolla
8. Jota Jota
8A. J.J. Left

9. Tirili
10. Perona
11. Chanco
12. No Cal Senior Fiscal

bend and enter the field at a rickety gate. Do not go up the track, marked as private, but bear left through the almond orchards into a shallow valley with a small crag containing a few routes well hidden in the trees on the left.

These include an E2 5c on the right and three very tough pitches on the left.

The main cliff is ten minutes walk further up the valley and is completely hidden from the road.

The routes are described from RIGHT to LEFT as this is the normal approach direction. The first three routes start from a ledge six feet up, below and right of a stout pine tree that sprouts from the solid rock 25 feet from the ground.

CALENAURA INVEVNAL   *   HVS   50ft.
The easiest route on the crag and a pleasant introduction to the style of climbing.
Step right past a substantial thread then follow the vague rib by sustained moves on excellent holds to the belay. Lower off.

EL ULTIMODELA FILA   **   E1   5b   55ft.
The central line on this section of wall gives good climbing with quite a tough crux. Climb straight up the wall to a small red bulge that is passed right then back left to reach big jugs and a little higher, the lowering stations.

PINCHITO MORUNA   *   E1   5b   55ft.
Perhaps rather easier than its near neighbour. Follow the line of bolts immediately to the right of the big tree on large holds to reach a shallow scoop. Entering and leaving this are tricky, but a short distance higher good holds lead away to the right to reach the belay of the previous route.
Above the three previous routes is an extension pitch that is somewhat steeper and harder than the ones below.

EXTENSION   ***   E2   5c   60ft.
Big holds lead up steep rock to a small "blank" scoop which is crossed

to a belay just above. Great climbing.

The next four routes climb the fine, steep grey slab to the left of the large pine growing from the rock. The right-hand line is:

EXTRA FINA ** E2 5c 50ft.
The line of bolts that trends slightly to the right and passes below some vegetation is followed to reach ledges and a lowering point. A sustained and fingery pitch.

CAGUERRA PERPETUA ** E1 5b 75ft.
This takes the right-most of the two bolt lines that shoot straight up the centre of the steep slab. It gives excellent sustained moves with as much protection as you could wish for and is fortunately rather easier than first appearances might suggest.

NAMELESS * E1 5b 80ft.
The left-hand line is slightly harder and makes straight for a conspicuous flake system at 60ft. Once this is reached move up then traverse to the right to reach the belay of the previous climb.

TU POLLA ME ENROLLA *** E2 5c 90ft.
A great pitch that takes the steepening wall just to the right of an area of flowstone. Tricky moves up the lower wall leads to the steepening. Step left and use 'chicken heads', (perhaps from the size of them they should be called 'turkey heads') to get established on the steeper rock. Above this spaced holds and spaced bolts lead ever upwards to the belay.

To the left the ground rises up and a great fallen flake is reached. The climbs in this area are steeper than the ones to the right but the protection fortunately is as good as ever. The next two routes start from atop the flake.

JOTA JOTA *** E3 5c 80ft.
Perhaps the best pitch on the crag with steep climbing on good holds, not high in the grade.

Step off the flake and climb the slab easily. Pull over the bulge leftwards on some hidden holds (if you can find them) then go directly up the steep wall above by intricate and sustained climbing. Superb.

JOTA JOTA LEFT ** E4 6a 80ft.
Not quite as majestic as the parent route but still well worthwhile.

Follow JOTA JOTA to its second bolt before moving left, or climb the straightforward but unprotected slab just to the left. Cross the bulge on small finger holds via a tough sequence then continue straight up the wall above, with more than enough protection and only just enough holds. The hardest pitch on the crag.

The next feature to the left is a corner crack formed by a flake. This is the start of:

TIRILI ** E3 5c 70ft.
Up the corner to the bulge which is crossed by pulling awkwardly to the right on to a hanging rib. Continue up the wall above on good holds to a second bulge which is passed to the right of the bolts by some strenuous moves. Before your strength evaporates completely continue up the still steep wall until it is possible to head left to the belay and salvation.

Between the flake corner and a large tree are two lines climbing a steep slab and continuing up steeper rock above. The right-hand line is:

PERONA ** E4 6a 70ft.
Up the steep slab with some difficulty until things begin to rear up. Step right, almost on the previous route then head slightly leftwards on small holds to a final steepening. Grapple with this to reach better holds (hopefully) and the belay of the previous route.

CHANCO *** E2 5c 80ft.
A great pitch, steep and unlikely.
Make difficult moves to pass the first bolt on the left-hand line then

99

continue more easily to a large pocket containing a miniature herb garden. Steep sustained moves now lead straight up the wall with a couple of blind pulls until relief arrives at some big holds. A swing right leads to easy ground which leads further to the right to reach the belay of the last two routes.

The final route on this section of the crag is to be found just around to the left of the large tree stood close to the rock.

NO CAL SENIOR FISCAL   ***   E1   5b   70ft.
Excellent sustained climbing, which is easier than it looks. Not difficult at the grade.

Climb the flake to the left of the initial bolt until it is possible to swing right to gain the line of the route. Once established here, welcome to the cruise, relax and enjoy the experience.

About 200m bushwhacking further up the valley is a domed buttress with four lines on it. These are unnamed and appear to be in the E1 to E3 category. Anyone bored with the climbing by numbers on the main crag could spend a happy hour or two here going back to their roots (or should it be routes?).

La Gubia

Character

La Gubia, normally referred to as simply Gubia, is Majorca's premier climbing area. It is basically an open ravine cutting deeply into the Sierra de Alfabia close to the town of Bunõla 15 km north of the centre of PALMA. The climbing is on a variety of cliffs scattered around the entrance to the gorge. Each cliff has its own atmosphere and faces in different directions allowing the sun to be followed or avoided depending upon the season and climatic conditions. Routes vary in height from 40ft up to 800ft and in difficulty from VS up to E "big numbers". The rock differs from cliff to cliff but is invariably excellent. Fixed gear is perfectly adequate on the majority of routes though some of the longer undertakings require a mixed rack; these are pointed out in the text. Most of the climbs described are longer than 25m and so two ropes are needed to ensure a retreat.

From the gorge the outward views are excellent. The fruit orchards are in the foreground and the blue Mediterranean beyond, with the occasional big bird of prey circling high overhead and the tinkling of goat bells carrying up from the meadows. A beautiful place to climb or just soak up the atmosphere.

Access

NOTE: *The following directions must be followed closely to avoid access problems, it would be a great loss if this place was to become another CRAIG Y FORWEN.*

From PALMA follow the main road (the C711) northwards to BUNÕLA and SOLLER for 15 km. The crag becomes visible on the left after about 13 km. Immediately before the complex junction that provides a right turn into BUNÕLA is a small track on the left that doubles back towards the cliff. The third entrance on the right down this is a wide track leading to a farm, it is possible to park on the right side of this on rough ground.

Continue down the main track for ten minutes to the second of two rickety gates. Pass through this and immediately scramble up into

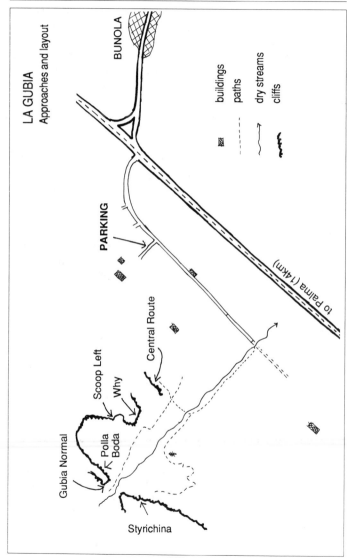

LA GUBIA
Approaches and layout

BUNOLA

PARKING

to Palma (14km)

Central Route

Scoop Left
Why

Polla
Boda

Gubia Normal

Styrichina

buildings
paths
dry streams
cliffs

the field on the right (on the other side of the dry stream bed). Follow a vague track that improves gradually, through fields of almost Biblical stoniness, up into the olive orchards and so in to the gorge. The path scrambles up to the right out of the stream bed and soon reaches a flat area that makes an ideal base, and possible bivi-site 20 minutes from the car. A little further on at the same level is a secluded dell that contains a neolithic table and chairs, the ideal place for the picnic you have been planning.

The individual areas are described from RIGHT to LEFT looking into the gorge. The first area of interest is a steep slabby wall directly above the point where the approach path scrambles out of the stream bed. The three routes here are described from LEFT to RIGHT as they are passed walking up the hillside.

LEFT-HAND ROUTE   *   E3   6a   40ft.
The first bolt ladder protects thin fingery climbing up a steepening slab. It is usual to lower off the fifth bolt using the in-situ mallion, though the bolt ladder continues until it loses itself in the exotic scrub at the top of the buttress.

CENTRAL ROUTE   *   E1   5b   60ft.
Starts by the large tree stood close to the crag below a line of paired bolts.
The lower slippery slab leads to a steeper section. The big chalked-up pocket is a red herring, so step left and sprint up the wall using a variety of side pulls to gain the niche containing the belays.

RIGHT-HAND ROUTE   *   E2   5c   60ft.
A short distance above the dry stone wall is another bolt ladder. The lower section is reasonable until the rock rears up at a bulge. There are two possibilities, either power straight on up to a huge jug before swinging right (it is probably easier to do the crux, then clip the protection bolt from the jug), or make a fingery traverse to the right and pull straight up to the belay. The latter method is technically harder but a bit less beefy; take your choice.
    The next section of rock to be described is the imposing red barrel-

103

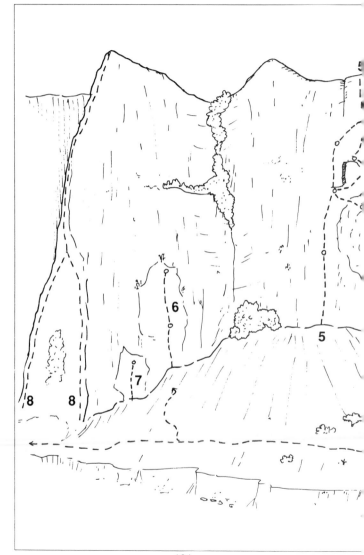

GUBIA NORTH WALL
A Panorama

1. Central route E1 *
2. Way E3 ***
3. Scoop Left E4 **
4. El Angel E1 ***
5. Princessa E4 ***
6. Polla Boda E2 **
7. Jodete Y Baila E2
8. Gubia Normal VS ***

shaped buttress that towers over the base camp area. A variety of rough tracks lead through the scrub to various parts of the buttress. The most prominent feature of this section of cliff is a central impressive crack line that does not reach the ground and has a prominent pod at half-height. This is the line of ZARAGUAI. Below this is an apron of more easy angled rock and the first routes start to the right of this. The routes are described from RIGHT to LEFT.

The wall is bounded by a steep gully, the side wall of which contains a couple of very impressive pitches. These are rumoured to be in the E6 category and they certainly look like it.

The left side of the wall has a slanting rake crossing it, this is the line of:

EXCALIBUR * HVS 5b 90ft.
Start by a giant tombstone shaped block and climb up onto the ramp. Follow it to the right to the base of a steep corner which provides the crux of the route. A little higher a stout tree provides an anchor for lowering off.

THE POCKETED WALL ** E5 6a 70ft.
Start just to the right of the easy corner that bounds the right side of the apron of easy rock. A smooth slab is climbed on good but painful holds until the rock begins to bulge and changes colour. Difficult and strenuous climbing leads up to bigger holds but not much change in angle. Those with stamina will press on to a good ledge and belays, but normal mortals may have to return to the ground for a breather before success is assured.

ZARAGUAI * E2 5c 80ft.
The imposing central crack of the buttress is approached up easier rock. Gaining the base of the crack constitutes the crux of the pitch and is done using small flakes or skinny finger jams. Once gained, the crack gives strenuous jamming and bridging, all very gritstonesque, until it is possible to move left to a good ledge and eight bolt belay.

Chris Craggs on Right-hand Route (E2 5c), La Gubia, Majorca

107

Immediately left of the crack of ZARAGUAI is a bubbly arête, this is:

FLYING BUTTRESS   *   E3   6a   80ft.
Climb ZARAGUAI until established in the crack. Now move left and swing boldly around the corner on to the impending face. This gives a series of strenuous moves on well-spaced holds until the angle eases, (the prominent hole through the arête is a total red herring, head for it at your own risk!). Now romp on to the belay.

WHY   ***   E3   6a   80ft.
The steep open corner on the left side of the buttress gives a fine technical pitch.
    Amble up easy rock to the corner then make awkward moves to get onto a boss. Swing on to the steep right wall then step back into the corner. A difficult rock-over leads to the final obstacle, a smooth bulging corner containing only one hold. Levitate up this then move right to the belay.

WHY LEFT   **   E4   6a   80ft.
Follow the parent route until a slanting crack leading away leftwards can be reached, this gives sustained strenuous and safe climbing to a set of sound anchors. Lower off.

Left of the open corner of WHY is a large red bulge taken centrally by:

BEEF IT   *   E5   6b   60ft.
The challenge is obvious, it makes you feel weak just looking upwards. If you feel up to it throw yourself at the overhangs, when some big holds, a lot of small holds and muscles in your spit may see you through.

Further to the left are more bulges from which hangs a prominent double thread. This marks the line of:

RHUMBA   *   E1   5b   120ft.
Climb an easy rib to the threads and pass them steeply to reach a ledge and possible stance. Climb the short wall (crux) to gain the steep groove which leads to an even steeper exit. Two bolt belay. To

descend traverse 20 feet to the left to reach the belay on the next route. The ground is 80 feet away.

The next two routes are to be found 50 metres further up the path lurking in a steep scoop, the back wall of which sprouts an unsightly growth.

SCOOP RIGHT   *   E3   6a   80ft.
A couple of desperate pulls on razor blades lead to and past the first bolt, (using a 'bunk up' is just not cricket). Once established, head straight up the steep wall avoiding any leanings to the right. A bulge is taken by laybacking to gain the easier upper slabs which are followed to the right to reach the belay.

SCOOP LEFT   **   E4   6a   80ft.
The finer twin. Bridge up the lower section easily until things begin to steepen up. From here a couple of desperate moves are made out to the right to reach a resting ledge. Any use of the flake on the left of the scoop reduces the route to V.Diff.! Swing back onto the rib and climb boldly up steep rock until better holds are reached. Step left and continue, still with interest to the belays.

The crag now falls back into a huge bay with a soaring south facing back wall riddled with caves. There are two major routes up this section of the cliff. The more amenable one is EL ANGEL, *** E1 5b. This consists of an eight pitch expedition that gains the prominent slanting ramp line from the left and follows it to its apex. From here it moves up and right to gain the right-most crack in the head wall. Take a standard UK rack.

DESCENT - As for GUBIA NORMAL.

Starting 30m further to the left and taking a direct line up steep grey rock is:

PRINCESSA   ***   E4   490ft.
A magnificent route, the best in the area and a must for 'any visiting

competent party.' Start at the highest point of the bay where a scratched arrow points to a small bush and belay bolts.

1.   160ft.   6a.   Climb up and left then follow the line of bolts and good holds straight up the impressive wall until it turns nasty (at a trio of bolts). A thin sequence reaches better holds and a little higher a small stance.

2.   110ft.   5b.   Head up and left past a bolt then climb directly up easier rock until it is possible to move right to a good ledge, complete with trees, below steeper rock.

3.   100ft.   5b.   Climb straight up behind the stance to the line of overhangs which are crossed on big holds to gain a fine wall. This is climbed moving gradually to the right to reach a foothold stance below a slanting groove.

4.   120ft.   5b.   Swing round the corner then traverse twenty five feet to the right before climbing straight up the fine wall to the top.

DESCENT. The route is equipped to allow an abseil descent back down the line of the route - gripping but quick. It is also possible to descend as for GUBIA NORMAL.

The penultimate area to be described on the right-hand side of the gorge is to be found just above the point where the sides of the ravine come close together and the path is squeezed close to the edge.

The lowest wall is a clean triangular piece of rock about 40ft high. This contains at least four minor routes, the most obvious of which is just right of centre. This is JODETE Y BAILA E2 5c. The other pitches are harder and rather less worthwhile.

A short distance up the slope to the right is a larger and less steep wall that contains some excellent pitches. All the routes on this face have a common first pitch starting at a well-trampled area at the base of the wall. From the top of all the second pitches it is possible to lower back to the ledge rather than use the rather cramped upper stances. The routes are described from LEFT to RIGHT.

LEFT ARETE ** HVS 140ft.

An excellent climb giving a good introduction to continental ethics.
1.   70ft. 5a.   Straight up the wall passing an awkward bulge at half-height before moving left to a rather meagre two-bolt belay. A somewhat harder start to the left is also possible though this may not be fully equipped.
2.   70ft. Rather harder 5a. Climb directly up from the stance on superb rock following the line of bolts; where these end continue in the same line with faith to the belay.

SOURISA VERTICAL * E1 140ft.

1.   70ft. 5a.   As for pitch one of LEFT ARETE but move right to a wire cable and bolt belay, and a stance guaranteed to tangle your ropes.
2.   70ft. 5b.   Climb up and left to pass the prominent bush then head straight up before bearing away left again by sustained moves with 'loadsa gear' to the stance.

POLLA BOBA ** E2 150ft.

1.   70ft. 5a.   As for pitch one of SOURISA VERTICAL to the cable belay.
2.   80ft. 5c.   Climb straight up the wall to a bulge that is passed with difficulty on to easier rock. Continue in the same vein to another steep section which gives a couple of tricky moves in a rather 'run out' situation to a large pocket. The final bulge is easier than the ones below due to the presence of a scattering of jugs; press on to the stance.

RIGHT ROUTE * E2 140ft.

1.   70ft. 5a.   As for pitch one of SOURISA VERTICAL to the cable belay.
2.   70ft. 5c.   From the stance bear slightly rightwards up the wall to reach a bulge containing some protuberances which are used to reach easier angled rock above (paired bolts, that will do very nicely, thank you). Spaced but good holds now lead without further fuss to the belay.

FAR RIGHT ROUTE * E3 140ft.

The most right-hand route on this section of the wall (at the moment).

1. 70ft. 5a. As for pitch one of SOURISA VERTICAL to the cable belay.

2. 70ft. 5c. Climb up and right keeping just to the right of the previous route until it is possible to swing right under a bulge. Cross this on small finger holds and continue up the scoop above until it becomes blocked. Swing up and then left with difficulty to reach the stance of the previous route.

The final feature on this side of the gorge is the soaring ridge that pierces the sky at the narrowest part of the ravine. This is LA GUBIA NORMAL *** VS 800ft. There are two starts to either side of the patch of red rock, the left one is 4b and the right one 4c, both are excellent. The left start is marked by a red cross and the right one by a hammered bolt head. The stances are all equipped (and numbered!) but there is not a great deal of fixed gear so carry a standard UK rack.

DESCENT. From the top of the climbing scramble up the ridge to the summit of the mountain. A path drops off the back to meet a good track which winds its way back down the mountain (passing a big dog on a long chain) to arrive at the Taverna a short distance north of where the car is parked. How very convenient.

The final section of LA GUBIA is the long and impressive wall on the left side of the gorge (looking upstream). This is the showcase of the area and contains some magnificent routes on superb rock and with excellent protection. The wall faces east and is in the sun until an hour or two after midday. All of the routes require two ropes, preferably 50m in length, to effect an easy retreat.

To reach the crag continue up the stream bed for 50m or so after the approach to the right side of the gorge, until below a conspicuous large solitary pine. Scramble up here keeping to the left of any rock until a good path leads up to the terraces below the cliff. A direct approach across from the right side of the gorge is best avoided because of the ravine, steep rock and vegetation.

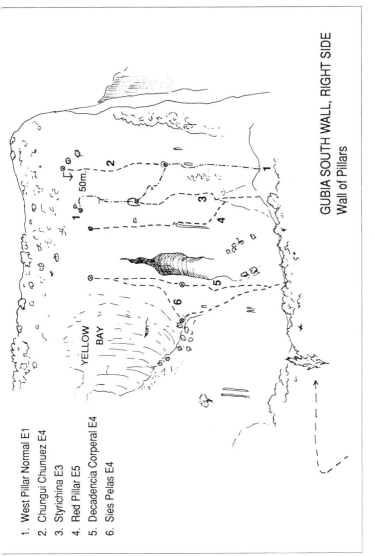

GUBIA SOUTH WALL, RIGHT SIDE
Wall of Pillars

1. West Pillar Normal E1
2. Chungui Chunuez E4
3. Styrichina E3
4. Red Pillar E5
5. Decadencia Corperal E4
6. Sies Pelas E4

113

The routes are described from RIGHT to LEFT, and the first two climbs are situated on the fine grey wall at the right extremity of the cliff. These are reached by scrambling up and right past bushes to reach a small hollow with a pair of bolts in it.

CHUNGUI CHUNUEZ *** E4 170ft.
A fine direct route with a superb second pitch.
1.   70ft.   5a.   From the twin bolts climb straight up the wall to a stance in a hollow with a substantial selection of belays.
2.   100ft.   6a.   Above the stance is a closely spaced line of bolts. Follow these easily at first then with more difficulty to a thread handhold. More difficult moves lead up and left to better holds in a steeper section of rock, continue straight up from here with the odd tricky move to eventually reach a good but very unusual set of belays. From here a pair of 50m ropes will just reach the ground: teams with 150ft ropes will have to split the descent and teams with a single 50m rope are in bother!

WEST PILLAR NORMAL   *** E1   200ft.
A great route taking the easiest line up a large wall. Start as for CHUNGUI CHUNUEZ at the hollow with twin bolts.
1.   70ft.   5a.   From the twin bolts climb straight up the wall on good holds heading for a white pillar, the top of which is one huge jug. Gain a standing position on this awkwardly and continue to a stance in a hollow with a substantial selection of belays.
2.   50ft.   5b.   Crossing the wall to the left is an obvious weakness, which is followed into the middle of nowhere. Move up then left, then up again (crux) to reach a hidden peg before swinging left into a cave where you can cower for a while. Chain and bolt belays.
3.   80ft.   5a.   Quite a serious pitch. Bridge out of the roof of the cave, spooky, and up on to the wall above. Climb up and right into a shallow groove and pull on to the wall above, which is climbed moving slightly right until it is possible to traverse left past a peg to a stout tree in a hole where there are a pair of chains through some chunky threads. Abseil descent but bear in mind the comments for the descent from the previous route.

114

The next feature to the left is a great tube that disappears upwards into the cliff. To the right of this is a magnificent wall that contains four routes. Below the wall is a grey apron of more easily angled rock; the first three routes start here.

STYRICHINA *** E3 5c 110ft.
Excellent, steep wall climbing on (mostly) good holds.

Climb easily up the grey apron (bolt) and move right in to a small bay containing a stunted bush at the foot of the steep part of the wall. Pull up and left before swinging awkwardly back right to gain a fretted pocket. Now climb straight up with difficulty to reach jugs, then continue in the same line avoiding the safety of the easier groove to the right until it is possible to bear away left, back towards the centre of the wall. Finish steeply into the cave with chains.

RIGHT WALL *** E5 6b 170ft.
Brilliant face climbing on tiny pockets.

Start as for the last route but continue straight up the apron and on to the intimidating wall. This gives fierce, fingery climbing on holds that are barely adequate until a slight easing in the angle gives respite. Continue with interest to a possible hanging stance, or press on up the fine grey wall above (6a) to where the route finally relents. Phew!

THE RED PILLAR *** E5 6a 170ft.
Another 'mega' pitch giving a scary outing up a 'drainpipe' glued to the wall.

Follow the last two routes to start before bearing left to the change in angle. Make difficult moves up left to reach the pillar. This can be climbed by laybacking, pinch gripping or like a monkey up a stick, or any combination of these that allows you to make progress. On top of the pillar is a bizarre rest before more steep wall climbing on small holds leads to a possible hanging stance. If you have not had enough, continue up the Verdon-like wall above (6a) or call up the second and send him up it.

The final route in this area climbs the leaning right wall of the 'black hole' on a series of pockets some of which are very large, though they are probably not large enough.

STAR TREK ** E6 6b 120ft.
Climb a groove below the right edge of the tube to a possible belay in bushes. From here climb the ever-steepening wall on pockets, to reach with luck and a modicum of ability, the belay. A mighty effort.

To the left of the 'black hole' is a fine grey pillar which is climbed by:

DECADENCIA CORPERAL *** E4 6a 90ft.
Climb up and right before swinging back left onto the pillar. This gives sustained climbing on poor pockets and small edges until it steepens and a sprint can be made to the belay chains. A second pitch is available (*** Hard E5 6b) for those who thought the first pitch was a pushover.

Further left the rock becomes rather scrappy until a smooth section with three weird lumps growing from it. To the right of these is a grey wall of rougher rock, this being:

SI LOSI NO VERGO ** E4 6a 70ft.
A short but enjoyable pitch on good rock leads to a lowering point as the rock turns dirty.

To the left the crag continues for a considerably distance as a series of caves and leaning walls interspersed with fine grey pillars. The walls are often covered with flowstone (tufa), pillars and huge stalagmites and there are pieces of 'tat' hanging in some most impressive places. There is a whole series of routes here in the E4 to E7 category, the majority of which look magnificent. It is to be hoped that climbers operating at these grades can sort the area out for themselves. To anyone bored with 'Ravens snore' a week on here should be a tonic - go to it.

To this end only one route in this section is described here:

SUPER TOUREN *** E3 6a 80ft.

A superb steep pitch on the most unlikely set of holds. Towards the right side of the steepest part of the wall is an overhanging scoop leading to some large holes. Climb up into the scoop and leave it on the right to reach a large hanging lump. Battle past this to reach an overhang which is crossed to gain a ledge. Move left and then up the wall to reach the lowering station.

Other Areas

As mentioned in the introduction to Majorca, the total amount of rock available is immense. This varies from boulders through bigger boulders to 1000 foot-high sea cliffs and some very impressive mountain crags. In several areas there have been a few climbs produced and these may be worth a visit if you are in the area or if you fancy a change for half a day. In most of these areas the scope for new routing, either traditional style or sport style, is almost limitless.

The most interesting areas are described clockwise around the island starting from PALMA (See Map Page 93).

Puerto Pi

An area of excellent bouldering, and some pretty fair swimming, a short distance from the city. Head out of PALMA for a couple of kilometres on the coastal dual carriageway to the first junction. Turn off and cross over the main road heading up the hill towards the sea, (the Naval base is to your left). Park at a long left-hand bend where there is a break in the chain.

Do NOT leave any valuables in your car.

Scramble down the bank to reach the cliff which runs eastwards for a considerable distance. Although only 10 to 15 feet high, the outcrop provides good sport both vertical and horizontally, (the latter in two planes). When it gets too hot or your hands can't take any more, take the plunge.

Valdemossa

A small collection of good routes in a gorgeous setting, they are in the sun after midday. From PALMA drive north for 14 km to the town of VALDEMOSSA. From here follow the road westwards towards ANDRAITX for a short distance to a right turn to PORT DE VALDE-MOSSA. Shortly after the road begins to descend there is parking by a large boulder. Fifty metres back up the hill is a pocketed wall rising directly from the tarmac, the ultimate road side crag, but keep your ears open for traffic. This contains five worthwhile routes. These are described from RIGHT to LEFT.

RIGHT RIB   *   E3   6a   60ft.
The right most line is a clean grey rib which is reached up a surprisingly tricky wall. Sustained and fingery.

RIGHT ROUTE   *   E1   5b   60ft.
To the left of a recess a steep start on big holds gains easier angled rock which leads leftwards onto the face. Fine climbing with a tricky couple of final moves gains the lowering bolts.

The final three routes on this wall share the same start and finish, though have independent middle sections.

RIGHT TRIPLET   E2   5c   60ft.
Gain a ledge at ten feet and swing right to follow the bolt ladder, steeply at first to the belay of the last route.

CENTRAL TRIPLET   *   E2   5c   60ft.
From the ledge climb straight up the sustained rib, the best of the trio.

LEFT TRIPLET   E2   5c   60ft.
The line is obvious, swing right to belay as for the other routes.

Further on down the road electricity cables pass overhead and there is parking on the right just beyond where the rock overhangs the road. There is one route here and this is also the parking place for the upper cliff.

ROADSIDE ATTRACTION   **   E3   6a   80ft.
Start from the road and climb the easy looking slab up and left to gain a rib. Continue up and left on good holds connected by difficult moves. A final steep section (crux) should see you hanging from the belay chains.

The final section of rock is to be found ten minutes rough scramble up and left from the car where a large open corner is found with a steep left wall and a slabby right wall. A lot of unclimbed rock is passed on the way to the cliff.

119

The routes are described from RIGHT to LEFT and descents are by abseil from any of the convenient trees.

SHORTY ** E1 120ft.
1. 70ft. 5b. At the right edge of the wall is a bulge. Climb over the bulge onto the face and continue straight up until tricky moves lead out left onto the slab. Continue straight up until stopped by bulges, then move right to a hanging stance, or more sensibly step down and right onto a ledge.
2. 60ft. 5a. Traverse right to a rib which is followed on a surprising set of holds to an overhang which is passed on the left to reach the top. Abseil descent.

LANKY ** E1 120ft.
Twenty feet right of the corner are a series of odd flutings, start at these.
1. 60ft. 5a. Climb the flutings then move out left before climbing straight up to a belay on threads and bolts. There is no stance and it might be better to press on.
2. 70ft. 5b. Gain the undercuts by the threads (crux) then move right into a corner. Continue up and out right across the lip of the roof to gain the open rib and an easier exit. Abseil descent.

To the left of the corner is a thin overhanging crack.

CRANK IT *** E5 6b 110ft.
The crack line starts off amenably enough but turns mean as height is gained. Desperate moves are made to reach the roof then better holds (if you can use them) lead to an eventual easing in angle. Belay or press on to the top, up the fine slab (5a). This excellent top pitch can be done as a route (HVS) by abseiling into the stance above the lower pitch.

Left again is a wide crack that steepens as it rises. This is:
LAYBACK * E3 5c 100ft.
Grovel up the initial wide rift then layback the imposing flake. At its top swing left and gain a ledge (possible belay) by a tricky move. Step

left then swing back right to climb a rib, making strenuous use of a tree. A belay and abseil point is available a short distance below the cliff top.

Further to the right are two lines that are obviously over desperate, do them if you can.

Alaro

A number of rather short routes on a collection of boulders (some of them pretty big) and some very impressive cliffs of excellent-looking rock.

From PALMA follow the main drag (C713) across the island to CONSELL (18 km). Turn left here to the quaint old town of ALARO (5 km) and follow signs for ORIENT. A few kilometres up here are a scattering of boulders on both sides of the road up to 40ft high and containing bolt-protected routes up to 6b. The main attraction of the area is, however, the mighty cliffs up the hill, which defend the ancient castle. These are approachable (at least in a hire car) by a road that degenerates into a rough track, starting at the 13 km marker stone back down the hill from the boulders. A path leads up to and through the base of the cliff, all very impressive stuff.

Cala de la Calobra

An area with virtually no development but bags of scope.

From the coast road between SOLLER and POLLENSA a tortuous road descends past plenty of impressive rock to a car park at sea level. This is worth a visit to experience the feat of engineering and to sample the sea level bouldering. There is a mass of excellent rock here ripe for new routing. Passing through the tunnel reveals more rock and the end of the classic gorge walk, the Torrente de Pareis, which starts way up the hill at ESCORCA.

In winter the trip down this ravine is a classic epic, 2 miles Moderate ***, (or at least E5 6b if you cannot swim). In summer it dries out and becomes a popular outing for old ladies in high-heels and gentlemen with doggies.

The Boquer Valley (or sometimes spelt Boca)

From behind PUERTO POLLENSA the Boquer valley runs out to sea. It is approached via the castle-like Boquer farm which lies at the end of a tree-lined avenue in a new housing development at the eastern end of PUERTO POLLENSA. Pass in front of the farm and take the right-hand gate. A little further on is a mass of boulders that the path weaves through (although called boulders many of then are larger than the average British crag). This is 15 minutes from the road.

The north side of the boulder to the left of the path has three bolt-protected routes which are 70ft. E4 6a to E5 6b (**) complete with chiselled finger holds (a good place to come and get some secret practise for the next competition) while excellent though rough bouldering is available scattered around the whole area.

A little further on it is possible to scramble up to the 'sharks fin' of rock that protrudes from the ridge above on the right. Below this is a big rounded boulder that contains two routes, 50ft. HVS 5b (*) with a common start up a bulging wall on big jugs. On the crag behind the boulder there is a VS 4b (***) in two pitches starting at the prominent crack (carry a few nuts) and two harder routes to the right. The left-hand one is E4 6a (**) and has a tough start to a ramp that is followed left on to a steep wall before moving right to a lowering point. The right-hand line is E3 5c (**) and gives a direct line providing steep sustained climbing on rock that is oh so sharp.

The cliffs to the left and right await development, while a kilometre or so up the valley is a huge crag that might repay a visit by anyone in search of an alpine epic without all that nasty white stuff.

Formentor

The headland that runs north-east from POLLENSA has some impressive cliffs though little appears to have been done. There are two areas of special interest.

Firstly, 6 kilometres out of town is a parking place on the left at MIRADOR. A footpath leads out a short distance to an impressive look-out. Directly below this path is a 200ft wall of excellent-looking rock - access could not be simpler.

Finally, 8 kilometres further on towards the lighthouse at CABO FORMENTOR the road passes through a tunnel bored through a huge cliff, the central part of which overhangs considerably. Further to the right the crag is shorter and the angle rather more amenable. As usual the rock looks great.

NOTES

Christina Howes
& Toni Mengual.

(climbers near Montserrat & Pedraforca)

66. Francesc Masià.

Vila de cavalls

TERRASSA.

BARCELONA.

(From Feb '93)

785 77 62 . (Toni's Work numb

CICERONE GUIDES

Cicerone publish a wide range of reliable guides to walking and climbing in Europe

FRANCE
TOUR OF MONT BLANC
CHAMONIX MONT BLANC - A Walking Guide
TOUR OF THE OISANS: GR54
WALKING THE FRENCH ALPS: GR5
THE CORSICAN HIGH LEVEL ROUTE: GR20
THE WAY OF ST JAMES: GR65
THE PYRENEAN TRAIL: GR10
TOUR OF THE QUEYRAS
ROCK CLIMBS IN THE VERDON

FRANCE / SPAIN
WALKS AND CLIMBS IN THE PYRENEES
ROCK CLIMBS IN THE PYRENEES

SPAIN
WALKS & CLIMBS IN THE PICOS DE EUROPA
WALKING IN MALLORCA
BIRDWATCHING IN MALLORCA
COSTA BLANCA CLIMBS

FRANCE / SWITZERLAND
THE JURA - Walking the High Route and
  Winter Ski Traverses

SWITZERLAND
WALKS IN THE ENGADINE
THE VALAIS - A Walking Guide
THE ALPINE PASS ROUTE

GERMANY / AUSTRIA
THE KALKALPEN TRAVERSE
KLETTERSTEIG - Scrambles
WALKING IN THE BLACK FOREST
MOUNTAIN WALKING IN AUSTRIA
WALKING IN THE SALZKAMMERGUT
KING LUDWIG WAY

ITALY
ALTA VIA - High Level Walkis in the Dolomites
VIA FERRATA - Scrambles in the Dolomites
ITALIAN ROCK - Selected Rock Climbs in
  Northern Italy
CLASSIC CLIMBS IN THE DOLOMITES

OTHER AREAS
THE MOUNTAINS OF GREECE - A Walker's
Guide
CRETE: Off the beaten track
Treks & Climbs in the mountains of RHUM &
PETRA, JORDAN
THE ATLAS MOUNTAINS

GENERAL OUTDOOR BOOKS
LANDSCAPE PHOTOGRAPHY
FIRST AID FOR HILLWALKERS
MOUNTAIN WEATHER
MOUNTAINEERING LITERATURE
SKI THE NORDIC WAY
THE ADVENTURE ALTERNATIVE

CANOEING
SNOWDONIA WILD WATER, SEA & SURF
WILDWATER CANOEING
A CANOEIST'S GUIDE TO NORTHERN
  ENGLAND (East)

CARTOON BOOKS
ON FOOT & FINGER
ON MORE FEET & FINGERS
LAUGHS ALONG THE PENNINE WAY

*Also a full range of guidebooks
to walking, scrambling, ice-climbing,
rock climbing, and other adventurous
pursuits in Britain and abroad*

CICERONE

*Other guides are constantly being added to the Cicerone List.
Available from bookshops, outdoor equipment shops or direct (send for price list)
from CICERONE, 2 POLICE SQUARE, MILNTHORPE, CUMBRIA, LA7 7PY*

CICERONE CLIMBING BOOKS

WINTER CLIMBING
WINTER CLIMBS IN THE LAKE DISTRICT *Bennett/Birkett*
WELSH WINTER CLIMBS *Campbell/Newton*
WINTER CLIMBS BEN NEVIS & GLENCOE *Grindley*
CAIRNGORMS, Winter Climbs *Fyffe*
MODERN SNOW & ICE TECHNIQUES *March*

ROCK CLIMBING: BRITAIN
ROCK CLIMBS, LANCASHIRE & THE NORTH WEST *Kelly/Cronshaw*
ROCK CLIMBS IN THE WEST MIDLANDS *Kerr*
THE ISLAND OF RHUM A Guide for Walkers, Climbers
    and Visitors *Brown*
MODERN ROPE TECHNIQUES *March*

ROCK CLIMBING: ABROAD
ROCK CLIMBS IN THE VERDON: An Introduction *Newcombe*
ITALIAN ROCK. Selected Climbs in Northern Italy *Churcher*
CLASSIC CLIMBS IN THE DOLOMITES *Dinoia/Casari*
TREKS AND CLIMBS Rum and Petra JORDAN *Howard*
Walks and Climbs in the PICOS DE EUROPA *Robin Walker*
COSTA BLANCA ROCK *Craggs*
ROCK CLIMBS IN THE PYRENEES *Derek L. Walker*

SCRAMBLES
SCRAMBLES IN THE LAKE DISTRICT *Evans*
MORE SCRAMBLES IN THE LAKE DISTRICT *Evans*
SCRAMBLES IN SNOWDONIA *Ashton*
SCRAMBLES IN LOCHABER *Williams*
SCRAMBLES IN SKYE *Parker*
VIA FERRATA SCRAMBLES IN THE DOLOMITES *Frass/Höffler/Werner*
KLETTERSTEIG Scrambles in the Northern Limestone Alps *Werner*

ALSO An extensive range of walking guides to many popular
areas of Britain, Europe and the Mediterranean countries.

AVAILABLE FROM YOUR OUTDOOR EQUIPMENT SHOP, BOOK-
SHOPS, OR DIRECT (Send s.a.e. for price list) from:
CICERONE PRESS 2 POLICE SQUARE, MILNTHORPE, CUMBRIA,
LA7 7PY Telephone: 05395 62069

Printed in Gt. Britain by
CARNMOR PRINT & DESIGN
95-97 LONDON RD. PRESTON